# Mastering BeagleBone Robotics

Master the power of the BeagleBone Black
to maximize your robot-building skills and
create awesome projects

**Richard Grimmett**

BIRMINGHAM - MUMBAI

# Mastering BeagleBone Robotics

First published: December 2014

Production reference: 1161214

Published by Packt Publishing Ltd.
Livery Place
35 Livery Street
Birmingham B3 2PB, UK.

ISBN 978-1-78398-890-7

www.packtpub.com

# Credits

**Author**
Richard Grimmett

**Reviewers**
Shantanu Bhadoria
Marcelo Boá
Chris J Daly
Daniel Frenzel
Brian C. Tomlinson

**Commissioning Editor**
Amarabha Banerjee

**Acquisition Editor**
Sam Wood

**Content Development Editor**
Prachi Bisht

**Technical Editor**
Humera Shaikh

**Copy Editor**
Vikrant Phadkay

**Project Coordinator**
Sageer Parkar

**Proofreaders**
Maria Gould
Clyde Jenkins
Elinor Perry-Smith

**Indexer**
Rekha Nair

**Graphics**
Sheetal Aute
Valentina D'silva
Abhinash Sahu

**Production Coordinator**
Manu Joseph

**Cover Work**
Manu Joseph

# About the Author

**Richard Grimmett** has always been fascinated by computers and electronics from his very first programming project that used Fortran on punch cards. He has a Bachelor's and a Master's degree in Electrical Engineering and a PhD in Leadership Studies. He also has 26 years of experience in electronics and computers and has one of the original brick phones and a Google Glass. He currently teaches computer science and electrical engineering at Brigham Young University, Idaho, where his office is filled with many of his robotic projects. He recently completed a book on using the Arduino for robotic projects, and another on the Raspberry PI.

I would certainly like to thank my wife, Jeanne, and family for providing me with a wonderful, supportive environment that encourages me to take up projects like this one. I would also like to thank my students who have shown me that amazing things can be accomplished by those who are unaware of the barriers.

# About the Reviewers

**Shantanu Bhadoria** is an avid traveler, Perl expert, and CPAN author based in Singapore. He has traveled to more than 30 countries around the world. When in Singapore, he works on paging and building control systems for skyscrapers and large campuses in Singapore, Hong Kong, and Macau. He has authored many libraries in Perl for control of gyroscopes, magnetometers, accelerometers, altimeters, PWM wave generators, and many other sensors and controllers.

He is also the author of Device::SMBus, a Perl library that is used to talk to devices over the I2C bus, and Math::KalmanFilter, a Perl library that implements the Kalman Filter sensor fusion algorithm.

His Perl code can be accessed at `https://metacpan.org/author/SHANTANU`, and his GitHub repositories are available at `https://github.com/shantanubhadoria`.

**Marcelo Boá** is an electronics technician who has a Bachelor's degree in Information Systems. He has worked for 10 years in the field of electronic maintenance. He has also worked on Java development, Oracle PL/SQL, PHP, ZK Framework, Shell scripts, HTML, JavaScript, Ajax, Linux, Arduíno, and BeagleBone.

He started as a PL/SQL trainee at the Federal Technological University of Paraná, Brazil. When the electronics technical department was formed, he worked for some companies on many different kinds of electronic circuits, thereby gaining technical assistance from Sony, Aiwa, and Gradiente. Ten years later, he returned to Java development with the ZK Framework, developing software for call centers in Curitiba's Software Park. He is currently working as a systems analyst in the warehouse management systems and industrial automation department at SSI SCHAEFER. He is an Arduíno and BeagleBone lover.

> This was my first experience as a reviewer and the experience was very good. The book is amazing. There are a lot of skills to learn from it.
>
> I would like to thank God for everything. I would also like to thank Sageer and Prachi for the invitation to join the book as a reviewer, and my family for allowing my training.

**Chris J Daly** lives near Portland, Oregon. During the day, he works as a software engineer, and in the evening, he spends time on hacking the Internet of Things projects, which can be found on his GitHub page at `https://github.com/cjdaly`.

**Daniel Frenzel** is a biochemist and biophysicist, and was working as a research associate at Forschungszentrum Jülich. Recently, he got a job offer from the EMBL in Heidelberg, where he will participate in the development of microfluidic systems. Daniel has experience in parallelization with OpenMP and CUDA under supercomputing conditions. He developed a C++ library for simulation of large-scale networks (`code.google.com/p/annetgpgpu`). Besides, Daniel maintains a quadcopter project based on the ArduPilot library, which allows him to control a quadcopter via WiFi (`code.google.com/p/rpicopter`).

# www.PacktPub.com

## Support files, eBooks, discount offers, and more

For support files and downloads related to your book, please visit www.PacktPub.com.

Did you know that Packt offers eBook versions of every book published, with PDF and ePub files available? You can upgrade to the eBook version at www.PacktPub.com and as a print book customer, you are entitled to a discount on the eBook copy. Get in touch with us at service@packtpub.com for more details.

At www.PacktPub.com, you can also read a collection of free technical articles, sign up for a range of free newsletters and receive exclusive discounts and offers on Packt books and eBooks.

https://www2.packtpub.com/books/subscription/packtlib

Do you need instant solutions to your IT questions? PacktLib is Packt's online digital book library. Here, you can search, access, and read Packt's entire library of books.

## Why subscribe?

- Fully searchable across every book published by Packt
- Copy and paste, print, and bookmark content
- On demand and accessible via a web browser

## Free access for Packt account holders

If you have an account with Packt at www.PacktPub.com, you can use this to access PacktLib today and view 9 entirely free books. Simply use your login credentials for immediate access.

# Table of Contents

# Preface

Robotics, the art and science of building machines that can perform some of the same functions as humans or animals, has been a part of human creative ambition since the time of the Greeks, who conceived Talos — a warrior made entirely of bronze that protected their lands and people. Leonardo da Vinci designed a mechanical knight that could sit, stand, and raise its visor. The first *modern* robots emerged in the 1920s — robots that could perform the same sort of simple motions as da Vinci's mechanical man through the use of electrical motors and signals.

In recent times, advances in technology have pushed the development of robots to the point of reality. Most of these projects have been created in defense department laboratories and university research facilities. However, new developments in inexpensive hardware and open source software have created opportunities for almost anyone to construct and experiment with automated machines.

The purpose of this book is not only to facilitate but also inspire these kinds of efforts. Robotics is no longer reserved for the PhD or even the trained engineer. You — yes, you — can construct machines that can roll, walk, swim, and even fly with the kind of functionality that is normally associated with intelligent life. I often tell my students that while they laugh at me because I once had to wash dishes by hand, their children will laugh at them because they had to load and unload the dishwasher by hand.

So, off to building the next great robotic breakthrough!

# What this book covers

*Chapter 1, Preparing the BeagleBone Black,* teaches you how to unbox, power up, and load the BeagleBone Black with all of the necessary software to build the projects described in this book.

*Chapter 2, Building a Basic Tracked Vehicle,* describes your first project, that is, a tracked vehicle. You'll learn how to construct the platform so that you can control the speed and direction of your robot.

*Chapter 3, Adding Sensors to Your Tracked Vehicle,* explains how, after creating a platform that is mobile, you'll add sensors to help your robot avoid, or find, objects.

*Chapter 4, Vision and Image Processing,* shows that your robot is maneuverable, but now you'll add the capability to not only sense but also see the world around it.

*Chapter 5, Building a Robot that Can Walk,* teaches you to build a robot that can walk—a quadruped robot controlled by the BeagleBone Black.

*Chapter 6, A Robot that Can Sail,* proves that while a robot that can roll or walk is impressive, one that can sail is even more amazing. You'll build a robot that can sail under the control of the BeagleBone Black.

*Chapter 7, Using GPS for Navigation,* shows that sailing your sailboat is easy if a human is controlling it. You can give your sailboat autonomy by giving it a sense of where it is and where it is going. The GPS system provides this feature and you'll learn how to use it to sail.

*Chapter 8, Measuring Wind Speed – Integrating Analog Sensors,* teaches you that to sail your sailboat, you'll need to know the wind direction. You'll learn how to use an anemometer (wind sensor) to sail your boat.

*Chapter 9, An Underwater Remotely Operated Vehicle,* demonstrates the construction of a vessel that can be controlled from the surface while it explores the environment under the water.

*Chapter 10, A Quadcopter,* shows that, now that you've explored the earth and the water, there is only one more place left to go—the air. You'll learn how to construct one of the most stable and maneuverable flying platforms—the quadcopter.

*Chapter 11, An Autonomous Quadcopter,* covers the final step in exploring the heavens, that is, providing your quadcopter with the capability of flying itself.

# What you need for this book

Generally, each chapter will detail the hardware and software needed for that chapter. However, before you get started, you'll need a BeagleBone Black, a host computer (Windows, Linux, or Mac), and an Internet connection for your BeagleBone Black, probably through some sort of LAN cable.

# Who this book is for

If you want a simple guide to building complex robots, then this book is for you. You'll need some programming knowledge, and experience of working with mechanical systems.

# Conventions

In this book, you will find a number of styles of text that distinguish between different kinds of information. Here are some examples of these styles, and an explanation of their meaning.

Code words in text, database table names, folder names, filenames, file extensions, pathnames, dummy URLs, user input, and Twitter handles are shown as follows: "Since the make system already knows how to build the `pocketsphinx_continuous` program, any time you make a change to the `continuous.c` file, it will rebuild the application."

Any command-line input or output is written as follows:

```
storage = cv.CreateMemStorage(0)
```

New terms and important words are shown in bold. Words that you see on the screen, in menus or dialog boxes for example, appear in the text like this: "Go to the **WIFI Adapters** section to see some devices that others have successfully used."

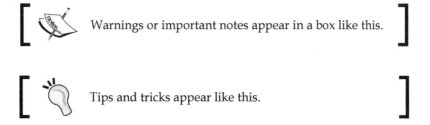

Warnings or important notes appear in a box like this.

Tips and tricks appear like this.

# Reader feedback

Feedback from our readers is always welcome. Let us know what you think about this book—what you liked or may have disliked. Reader feedback is important for us to develop titles that you really get the most out of.

To send us general feedback, simply send an e-mail to feedback@packtpub.com, and mention the book title via the subject of your message.

If there is a topic that you have expertise in and you are interested in either writing or contributing to a book, see our author guide on www.packtpub.com/authors.

# Customer support

Now that you are the proud owner of a Packt book, we have a number of things to help you to get the most from your purchase.

# Downloading the example code

You can download the example code files for all Packt books you have purchased from your account at http://www.packtpub.com. If you purchased this book elsewhere, you can visit http://www.packtpub.com/support and register to have the files e-mailed directly to you.

# Downloading the color images of this book

We also provide you a PDF file that has color images of the screenshots/diagrams used in this book. The color images will help you better understand the changes in the output. You can download this file from: https://www.packtpub.com/sites/default/files/downloads/8907OS_Graphics.pdf.

# Errata

Although we have taken every care to ensure the accuracy of our content, mistakes do happen. If you find a mistake in one of our books—maybe a mistake in the text or the code—we would be grateful if you would report this to us. By doing so, you can save other readers from frustration and help us improve subsequent versions of this book. If you find any errata, please report them by visiting http://www.packtpub.com/submit-errata, selecting your book, clicking on the **errata submission form** link, and entering the details of your errata. Once your errata are verified, your submission will be accepted and the errata will be uploaded on our website, or added to any list of existing errata, under the Errata section of that title. Any existing errata can be viewed by selecting your title from http://www.packtpub.com/support.

# Piracy

Piracy of copyright material on the Internet is an ongoing problem across all media. At Packt, we take the protection of our copyright and licenses very seriously. If you come across any illegal copies of our works, in any form, on the Internet, please provide us with the location address or website name immediately so that we can pursue a remedy.

Please contact us at copyright@packtpub.com with a link to the suspected pirated material.

We appreciate your help in protecting our authors, and our ability to bring you valuable content.

# Questions

You can contact us at questions@packtpub.com if you are having a problem with any aspect of the book, and we will do our best to address it.

# 1
# Preparing the BeagleBone Black

The BeagleBone Black, with its low cost and amazing package of functionalities, provides an excellent set of core functionalities to build robotic projects. In this book, you'll build three robotics projects, each with a differing array of fascinating functionalities. Hopefully, these will inform and inspire you so that you'll feel comfortable creating your own dream projects in robotics.

But let's not get ahead of ourselves. In this book, I'm going to assume quite a bit of knowledge of not only the BeagleBone Black, but also programming in general and specifically Linux. If you're truly a beginner, you'll have to start with my other book on the BeagleBone Black, *BeagleBone Robotic Projects*, *Packt Publishing*. However, I'm not going to assume that you've read the other book, so this first chapter will lead you through, in an accelerated way, the steps you'll need to follow from unpacking to having a BeagleBone Black that is configured to be successful in building complex robotics projects. To understand this book, you'll also need a bit more knowledge of how to connect electronic devices. You'll use the **General-Purpose Input/Output (GPIO)** pins and even a soldering iron to build these robots.

In this chapter, you will learn about the following:

- Installing an operating system
- Installing a vision library and sound capabilities
- Creating and recording sounds
- Making your BeagleBone speak
- Installing speech recognition
- Improving accuracy of speech recognition
- Adding additional hardware and software for a fully functional core system

So let's start with unpacking our BeagleBone Black. For this chapter, you'll need the following hardware:

- A BeagleBone Black board
- A BeagleBone Black USB power cable
- A LAN cable
- A USB sound device that has a plug for a microphone and a speaker
- A microphone
- A speaker
- A USB Wi-Fi dongle (this is optional; needed if you want to communicate with the BeagleBone Black via a wireless LAN).

# Unpacking and powering up

Let's unpack the single-board computer hardware device. Your BeagleBone Black will come in a box—in a static protection bag, with a USB cable that can power the unit from a USB connection. It should look somewhat like this:

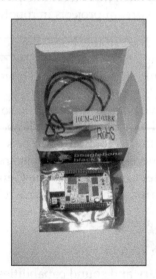

The USB connection not only supplies power to the host computer, but also provides a simple, yet fairly limited, way to communicate with the board. You'll use this USB cable for power, but that's about it.

You can also choose to power the BeagleBone Black using the 5 V barrel jack. One that works well is from Adafruit, available at `https://www.adafruit.com/products/276`.

If you've never worked with the BeagleBone Black before, the `beagleboard.org` site can lead you through the first few steps, from powering on to making sure your board is up and working, and to some initial communications with the board.

You must know that there are several versions of the board now. The latest, at the time of the writing of this book, is version C. The most significant change from Version B to Version C is that Version C has a 4 GB eMMC disk. Even this might be a bit small for your projects, and you're going to use an 8 GB to 16 GB micro SD card anyway, so either version should be fine.

# Installing an operating system

The first thing you need to do is install a useful operating system into an 8 GB, 16 GB, or 32 GB micro SD card—just a little background for this. Initially, the default operating system on the internal memory was a version of Linux called **Ångström**. Version C is now shipped with a version of **Debian**. You're going to move to a different operating system called **Ubuntu**, a close relative of Debian, but with a larger feature set and community of support. It'll make the projects you are about to tackle much easier.

Now the BeagleBone Black is getting popular enough, so you can buy a micro SD card that already has Ubuntu installed. Nevertheless, you can easily download it and then install it on the card. If you're going to download a distribution, you'll need to make sure you're getting the latest version of Ubuntu.

 The easiest way to download is to go to one of the several sites that have an image you can put on your card. One is at `www.armhf.com/boards/beaglebone-black/#saucy` and another is at `elinux.org/Beagleboard:Ubuntu_On_BeagleBone_Black`.

Both of these sites come with instructions for building a card with the image on it. You'll need to use the username and password of the image you downloaded. Unfortunately, they are not the same for all images, but you should be able to easily find them in the same place where you found your image.

# Connecting to an external computer

In this book, I'm going to assume that you'll be developing your code on an external computer while you create your projects. I'll primarily be using a Windows PC for development, but everything I'll be doing will also be available if you are using a Linux machine as the host computer. Whenever there are any significant differences between the two, I'll try to include details for both.

To do this development remotely, you'll need access to the BeagleBone Black via some type of LAN connection. To establish this connection, simply connect a LAN cable from a router or switch to the BeagleBone board, plug it into the LAN connector, and restart the BeagleBone.

> You can also use an FTDI console cable like the ones sold at https://www.adafruit.com/products/954, which are connected to the BeagleBone Black's J1 console UART pins.
>
> Refer the following link for details about setup: http://elinux.org/Beagleboard:BeagleBone_Black_Accessories

You'll need to know the IP address of your BeagleBone Black. You can certainly get this by adding a display and keyboard to the device, logging in, and typing ifconfig in the prompt. However, if you want to do this without rounding up the additional hardware, then you can use an IP scan tool to scan for the address of the BeagleBone Black. I used a tool called **Advanced IP Scanner**, but there are others available too. If you're using Linux as a host machine, you can try the nmap command in Linux. For example, you can type sudo nmap -PR -sP 192.168.1.0/24.

These will explore your network and then print the address where there are devices, the BeagleBone Black being one of those devices. Generally, there are two types of IP addresses that your board can be assigned: one is called **static** and the other is called **dynamic**.

In the static case, you will always be assigned the same address. In the dynamic case, the address might change each time the system boots, as it asks the system for an address, which it then uses for that session. Most systems are configured for the dynamic case. However, if your system isn't changing the address, you will most likely get the same address each time you power on and log in to the system.

To learn more about DHCP, visit www.teracomtraining.com/
tutorials/teracom-tutorial-dynamic-IP-addresses-
and-DHCP.htm.

Once you have the address, you should create an SSH connection to the BeagleBone Black. An **SSH** terminal is a **Secure Shell Hyperterminal** connection, which simply means that you'll be able to access your board and type commands in the prompt, just like you have done without the Windows system. In order to do this, you need to have a terminal emulator on your remote computer. For Microsoft Windows, I would suggest you to use an application called **PuTTY**. It is free and does a very good job by allowing you to save your configuration, so you don't have to type it every time. You can go to www.putty.org for details on how to download and use PuTTY.

If you want to do this from a Linux machine, the process is even simpler. Open a terminal window and then type ssh ubuntu@157.201.194.187 -p 22. This will then bring you to the login screen of your BeagleBone Black.

SSH is an excellent way to communicate with your BeagleBone Black. However, you'll sometimes need a graphical look at your system. You can get this by installing a graphical interface on the BeagleBone Black and then using an application called **VNC server**.

# Installing a Windows manager

First, let's install the Windows manager on your BeagleBone Black. Ubuntu generally comes with a very full-featured Windows system. However, it uses a good deal of memory and can interfere with the performance you might need later. So you should install a *light* Windows system at the top of your Ubuntu distribution. There are several choices, of which I like using **Xfce**. It is stable, seems to work well, and offers a fairly complete set of capabilities while not overwhelming your system resources. Before getting started, first type sudo apt-get update. This will update all the latest information about installation. To install the Windows manager, type sudo apt-get install xfce4. Again, the system will prompt you for your password and then start the installation. For large installations, the Linux system will ask you if you want to proceed. If you don't always want to type in y to this, you can use apt-get -y to automatically answer with a yes. This installation will take a significant amount of time as it has to install not only the Windows system, but also a number of packages the windowing system depends on.

Now that you have a graphical interface, you'll need to install a version of VNC server on your BeagleBone Black by typing `sudo apt-get install tightvncserver` in a terminal window on your BeagleBone Black. The **TightVNC server** is an application that will allow you to remotely view your complete Windows system. Once you have it installed, you'll need to start the server by typing `vncserver` in a terminal window on the BeagleBone Black. You will then be prompted for a password. This can, and preferably should, be a different password than the password using which you access your BeagleBone Black. This will be the password your remote system will send to access the VNC server running on the board. Select a password and your VNC server will be running. You only need to set this password once. Besides, you don't need to set the password for the view-only capability.

You'll need a VNC viewer application for your remote computer. On my Windows system, I used an application called **Real VNC**. Go to `www.realvnc.com` for information on how to set up and use this application. You can now access all the capabilities of your system. However they might be slower if you are doing graphics-intensive data transfers. You'll see this as you work through your projects. VNC viewer is also available via Linux.

You now have a basic BeagleBone Black configuration, so you can add some additional core packages you'll be using in the projects.

# Installing additional core software packages

The two packages that you'll add here are a core vision package called **OpenCV** and a core voice recognition package called **pocketsphinx**. It's up to you whether to use them or not, but allowing your robot to see, hear, and speak seems like it should be a part of any robotics project, so adding them now will make them easier to use later. Let's start with OpenCV.

First, when you created your SD card, you copied an image to your card. So now, your card thinks it is only the size of the image that you copied, no matter what size it really is. You'll need to reclaim this space.

To do this, you'll need to issue some fairly cryptic commands, but fortunately, you'll be able to use the defaults, so it will be straightforward. First, open a terminal window. The card I am using is an 8 GB card, so if your card is of a different size, don't be worried if you don't see the exact numbers as you see here. Fortunately, you'll be using default values throughout the process, so you won't need to know anything special about your card. To begin with, type `sudo su` and enter your password.

Then follow the following steps:

1.  Type `ll /dev/mmcblk*` and you should see something like this:

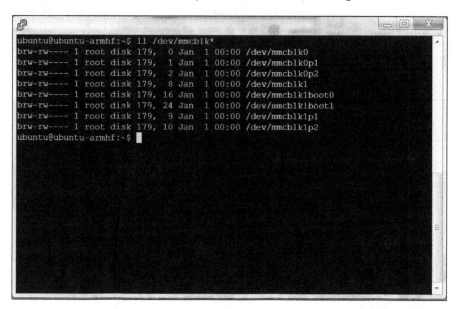

2.  Now you are going to make changes to the `mmcblk0` device. Type `fdisk /dev/mmcblk0`.

3.  Enter the `p` command and you should see something like this:

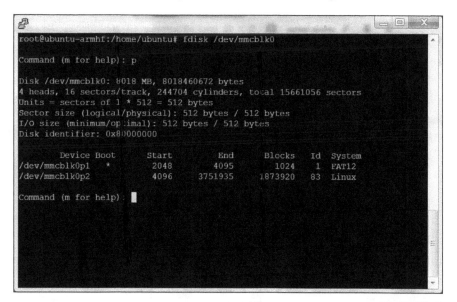

4. You're now going to expand the second device, /dev/mmcblk0p2. To do this, delete the partition and create a new partition. The information that exists on your SD card should, however, be preserved during this process. Enter d in the prompt and enter 2 for the second partition. Now enter p again and you should see something like this:

```
Sector size (logical/physical): 512 bytes / 512 bytes
I/O size (minimum/optimal): 512 bytes / 512 bytes
Disk identifier: 0x80000000

        Device Boot      Start         End      Blocks   Id  System
/dev/mmcblk0p1   *        2048        4095        1024    1  FAT12
/dev/mmcblk0p2            4096     3751935     1873920   83  Linux

Command (m for help): d
Partition number (1-4): 2

Command (m for help): p

Disk /dev/mmcblk0: 8018 MB, 8018460672 bytes
4 heads, 16 sectors/track, 244704 cylinders, total 15661056 sectors
Units = sectors of 1 * 512 = 512 bytes
Sector size (logical/physical): 512 bytes / 512 bytes
I/O size (minimum/optimal): 512 bytes / 512 bytes
Disk identifier: 0x80000000

        Device Boot      Start         End      Blocks   Id  System
/dev/mmcblk0p1   *        2048        4095        1024    1  FAT12

Command (m for help):
```

5. You will now create a new partition using defaults so that the partition takes up the entire card. In the command prompt, type n, then p, then 2, and then hit *Enter* through each choice that the programs request. Your device should now appear like this:

```
Partition type:
   p   primary (1 primary, 0 extended, 3 free)
   e   extended
Select (default p): p
Partition number (1-4, default 2): 2
First sector (4096-15661055, default 4096):
Using default value 4096
Last sector, +sectors or +size{K,M,G} (4096-15661055, default 15661055):
Using default value 15661055

Command (m for help): p

Disk /dev/mmcblk0: 8018 MB, 8018460672 bytes
4 heads, 16 sectors/track, 244704 cylinders, total 15661056 sectors
Units = sectors of 1 * 512 = 512 bytes
Sector size (logical/physical): 512 bytes / 512 bytes
I/O size (minimum/optimal): 512 bytes / 512 bytes
Disk identifier: 0x80000000

        Device Boot      Start         End      Blocks   Id  System
/dev/mmcblk0p1   *        2048        4095        1024    1  FAT12
/dev/mmcblk0p2            4096    15661055     7828480   83  Linux

Command (m for help):
```

Notice that the second partition is now much larger than the original.

6. Type w to commit your changes. Now you need to reboot, so type reboot.

7. The final step will expand the filesystem. After the system reboots, type sudo su and enter your password. Now type df. You should see something like this:

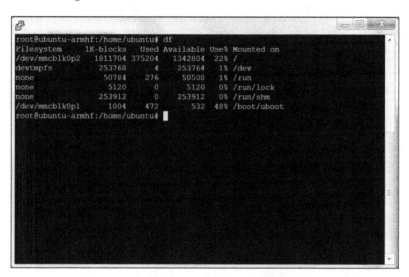

8. It's the /dev/mmcblk0p2 device that you want to resize. Type resize2fs / dev/mmcblk0p2 and then enter df. You should see the following:

```
root@ubuntu-armhf:/home/ubuntu# df
Filesystem      1K-blocks    Used Available Use% Mounted on
/dev/mmcblk0p2   1811704  375204   1342804  22% /
devtmpfs          253768       4    253764   1% /dev
none               50784     276     50508   1% /run
none                5120       0      5120   0% /run/lock
none              253912       0    253912   0% /run/shm
/dev/mmcblk0p1      1004     472       532  48% /boot/uboot
root@ubuntu-armhf:/home/ubuntu# resize2fs /dev/mmcblk0p2
resize2fs 1.42 (29-Nov-2011)
Filesystem at /dev/mmcblk0p2 is mounted on /; on-line resizing required
old_desc_blocks = 1, new_desc_blocks = 1
The filesystem on /dev/mmcblk0p2 is now 1957120 blocks long.

root@ubuntu-armhf:/home/ubuntu# df
Filesystem      1K-blocks    Used Available Use% Mounted on
/dev/mmcblk0p2   7678040  376572   6973284   6% /
devtmpfs          253768       4    253764   1% /dev
none               50784     276     50508   1% /run
none                5120       0      5120   0% /run/lock
none              253912       0    253912   0% /run/shm
/dev/mmcblk0p1      1004     472       532  48% /boot/uboot
root@ubuntu-armhf:/home/ubuntu#
```

Now that you have installed your operating system and expanded your storage device, your BeagleBone Black is ready to use.

# Installing a vision library

Now you'll install OpenCV, an open source library of image processing and a web camera that provides access capabilities you'll use on these projects.

First, you'll need to download a set of libraries and the OpenCV itself. There are several possible steps; I'm going to suggest one that I followed to install it on my system. Once you have booted the system and opened a terminal window, type the following commands in the same order as they have been explained:

1. `sudo apt-get install build-essential`: You are going to need this library as it provides a set of essential build tools.

2. `sudo apt-get install libavformat-dev`: This library provides a way to code and decode audio and video streams.

3. `sudo apt-get install libcv2.4 libcvaux2.4 libhighgui2.4`: These are the basic OpenCV libraries. Note the number at the end of each of these library specifications; this will almost certainly change as new versions of OpenCV become available. If Version 2.4 does not work, go to `opencv.org` to find the latest version of OpenCV.

4. `sudo apt-get install python-opencv`: This is the Python development kit for OpenCV. It is needed as you are going to use some Python code; it's the easiest language to use with this functionality.

5. `sudo apt-get install opencv-doc`: This is the documentation for OpenCV, just in case you need it.

6. `sudo apt-get install libcv-dev`: This provides a set of header files used to compile OpenCV.

7. `sudo apt-get install libcvaux-dev`: This provides a translator for certain tool sets.

8. `sudo apt-get install libhighgui-dev`: This provides a set of header files used to compile OpenCV, especially the GUI.

9. `cp -r /usr/share/doc/opencv-doc/examples`: Execute this command in your home directory; this will copy all the examples to your home directory.

Now you're ready to try out the OpenCV library. I prefer to use Python when programming simple tasks, so I used the Python examples. If you prefer the C examples, feel free to explore. In order to use the Python examples, you'll need one more library. So type `sudo apt-get install python-numpy` as you will need this to manipulate the matrices that OpenCV uses to hold the images you will get from your webcam.

Now that you have those, you can try one of the Python examples. Change the current directory to that of the Python examples by typing `cd /home/ubuntu/examples/python`. In this directory, you will find a number of useful examples; you only need to look at the most basic example, called `camera.py`. You can try running this example, but you'll need to connect a USB web camera, reboot, bring up a VNC server connection, bring up a terminal window, and type `python camera.py`. You should see something like this:

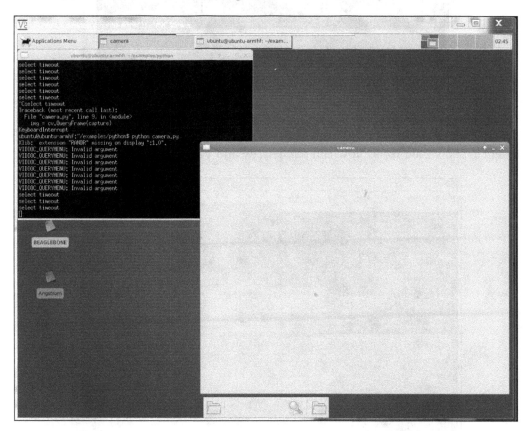

In my case, the camera window eventually turned black and did not show the output from the camera. I realized that I needed to change the resolution of the image to one that is supported by the camera and OpenCV. To do this, you need to edit the camera.py file, adding two lines like this:

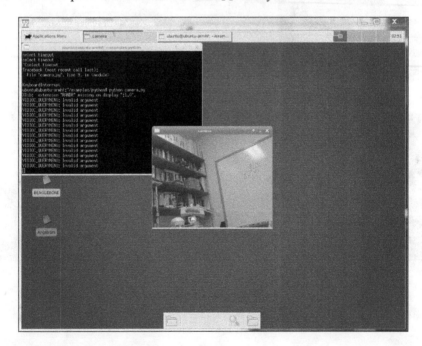

These two lines, cv.SetCaptureProperty(capture, 3, 360) and cv.SetCaptureProperty(capture, 4, 240), change the resolution of the captured image to 360 x 240 pixels. Now run camera.py and you should see this:

Your project can now see! You will use this capability to do a number of impressive tasks that will use this video input.

# Installing sound capability

The second piece of open source infrastructure that you'll add now is the voice recognition software—pocketsphinx. To make it work, you'll need to purchase a USB sound card, as the BeagleBone Black does not have an audio in/out provision. You'll also need to purchase a microphone and speaker to attach to your USB sound card. Connect these, and reboot the system. You're now ready to install the software.

You can do this over the LAN connection via an SSH terminal window, so as soon as your board flashes that it has power (look out for the heartbeat LED), open up an SSH terminal window using PuTTY or some similar terminal emulator. Once the terminal window comes up, log in with your username and password. Now type `cat /proc/asound/cards`. You should see the following response:

```
ubuntu@ubuntu-armhf: ~                                          _ □ ✕
login as: ubuntu
ubuntu@157.201.194.187's password:
Welcome to Ubuntu 12.04.2 LTS (GNU/Linux 3.8.13-bone20 armv7l)

 * Documentation:  https://help.ubuntu.com/
Last login: Sat Jan  1 00:03:11 2000 from grimmetr.c.byui.edu
ubuntu@ubuntu-armhf:~$ cat /proc/asound/cards
 0 [Black          ]: TI_BeagleBone_B - TI BeagleBone Black
                      TI BeagleBone Black
 1 [Device         ]: USB-Audio - USB PnP Sound Device
                      USB PnP Sound Device at usb-musb-hdrc.1.auto-1, full speed
ubuntu@ubuntu-armhf:~$ []
```

Notice that the system thinks there are two possible audio devices. The first is the HDMI sound device and the second is your USB audio card. Now you can use the USB card to both create and record sound.

# Creating and recording sound

First, let's get some music going. This will let you know that your USB sound device is working. You'll need to first configure your system to look for your USB card and play and record some sounds from there as default. To do this, you'll need to add a couple of libraries to your system:

1. The first are some ALSA libraries. **ALSA** stands for **Advanced Linux Sound Architecture**, but all you really need to know is that it enables your sound system on the BeagleBone Black. First, install two libraries associated with ALSA by typing `sudo apt-get install alsa-base alsa-utils`.

2. Then also install the library include files by typing `sudo apt-get install libasound2-dev`. This will install the basic capability that you need.

**Just a note**

Your system might already contain these libraries. If it does, then it won't hurt to try and install them; Linux will simply tell you that they are already installed.

3. Now you can use an application called **alsamixer** to control the volume of both the input and the output of your USB sound card. Type `sudo alsamixer` in the prompt. You should see a screen like this:

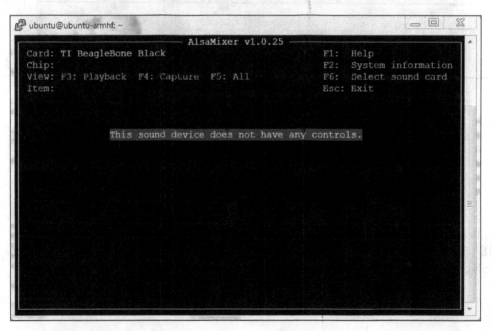

4. Press *F6*, and select your USB sound device using the arrow keys. The screen should now appear like this:

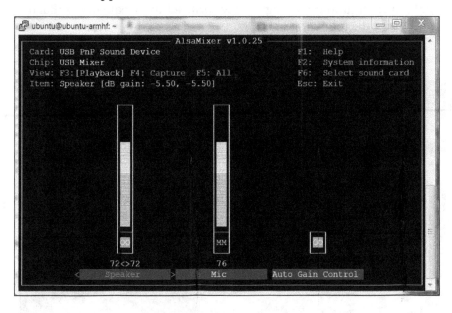

5. You can use the arrow keys to set the volume for both the speakers and the mic. Make sure you use the *M* key to unmute the microphone.

6. Now make sure that your system knows about your USB sound device. In the prompt, type sudo aplay -l. You should see the following:

```
ubuntu@ubuntu-armhf:~$ aplay -l
**** List of PLAYBACK Hardware Devices ****
card 0: Black [TI BeagleBone Black], device 0: HDMI nxp-hdmi-hifi-0 []
  Subdevices: 1/1
  Subdevice #0: subdevice #0
card 1: Device [USB PnP Sound Device], device 0: USB Audio [USB Audio]
  Subdevices: 1/1
  Subdevice #0: subdevice #0
ubuntu@ubuntu-armhf:~$ 
```

7. Once you have added the libraries, add a file to your home directory by the name .asoundrc. This will be read by your system and used to set your default configuration. Using your favorite editor, create the .asoundrc file and insert the following in it:

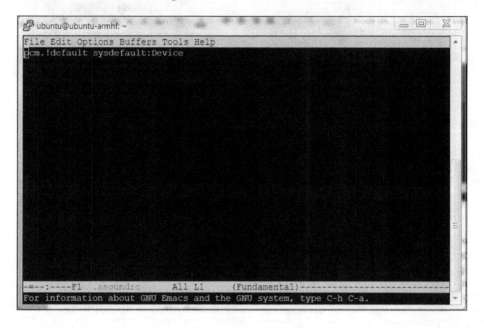

8. The line to be added is pcm.!default sysdefault:Device. This will tell the system to use our USB device as a default.

9. Once you have completed this, reboot your system.

10. Now that your system is ready, record some sound and play it. To do this, use the arecord program. In the prompt, type arecord -d 5 -r 48000 test.wav. This will record 5 seconds of a sound at a 48,000 sample rate.

11. Once you've typed the command, then either speak into the microphone or make some other recognizable sound. After 5 seconds, you should be able to play the sound.

12. Type aplay test.wav, and you should hear the recording of your voice.

If you can't hear your recording, check alsamixer to make sure your speakers and microphone are both unmuted.

# Making your BeagleBone Black speak

Now that you can get sounds both in and out of your BeagleBone Black, let's start doing something useful with this capability. Start by enabling **Espeak**, an open source application that provides you with a computer voice with a bit of personality. To get this functionality, download the Espeak library by typing `sudo apt-get install espeak`. You'll probably have to accept the additional size that the application requires, but this is fine based on your SD card size. This might take a bit of time to download, but the prompt will reappear when it is done.

Now let's see if your BeagleBone Black has a voice. Type the `sudo espeak "hello"` command. The speaker should emit a computer-voiced "hello." If it does not, make sure that the speaker is on and its volume is high enough to be heard. Now that you have a computer voice, you can customize it. Espeak offers a fairly complete set of customization features, including a large number of languages, voices, and other options.

Now your project can speak. Simply type `espeak`, followed by the text you want it to speak in quotes, and out comes your speech! If you want to read an entire text file, you can do that as well, using the `-f` option and then typing the name of the file. Try this by using your editor to create a text file called `speak`, then type this command: `sudo espeak -f speak.txt`.

# Installing speech recognition

Now that your projects can speak, you will want them to listen as well. This isn't nearly as simple as the speaking part, but thankfully you have some significant help. You will download a set of capabilities called **pocketsphinx**, and using these capabilities, you will provide your project with the ability to listen to your commands.

The first step is to download the pocketsphinx capability. Unfortunately, this is not as user friendly as the Espeak process, so follow the steps carefully. First, go to the Sphinx website, hosted by Carnegie Mellon University at `http://cmusphinx.sourceforge.net/`. This is an open source project that provides you with the speech recognition software you will need. With your smaller embedded system, you will be using the pocketsphinx version of this code. You will need to download two pieces of software, **sphinxbase** and **pocketsphinx**. Download these by selecting the **Download** section at the top of the page, and then find the latest version of both the packages. Download the `.tar.gz` versions of these and move them to the `/usr/ubuntu` directory of your BeagleBone Black. However, before you build these, you'll need another library.

This library is called **bison**. It's a general purpose, open source parser that will be used by pocketsphinx. To get this package, type `sudo apt-get install bison`.

If everything explained so far is installed and downloaded, you can build pocketsphinx as follows:

1.  Start by unpacking and building the sphinxbase. Type `tar -xzvf sphinx-base-0.x.tar.gz` where x is the version number. This should unpack all the files from your archive into a directory called `sphinxbase-0.x`. Now change to that directory.

2.  Now you will build the application. Start by issuing the `./configure --enable-fixed` command. This will first check to make sure everything is ok with the system, then configure a build. When I first attempted this command, I got the following error:

3.  This highlighted an interesting problem. The time and date on my BeagleBone Black was not set to the current time and date. If you need to set the current date and time, do that by issuing the `sudo date nnddhhmmyyyy.ss` command where nn is the month, dd is the day, hh is the hour, mm are the minutes, yyyy is the year, and ss is the second. This will set the date to the desired date. Now you can reissue the `./configure --enable-fixed` command.

4.  You can also install python-dev using `sudo apt-get install python-dev` and Cython using `sudo apt-get install cython`. Both of these will be useful later if you are going to use your pocketsphinx capability with Python as a coding language. You can also choose to install `pkg-config`, a utility that can sometimes help when you are trying to do complex compilations. Install it using `sudo apt-get install pkg-config`.

Now you are ready to actually build the sphinxbase code base. This is a two-step process. First type `make`, and the system will build all the executable files. Then type `sudo make install` and it will install all the executables on the system.

Now make the second part of the system, the pocketsphinx code itself, as follows:

1.  Go to the home directory and unarchive the code by typing `tar -xzvf pocketsphinx-0.x.tar.gz`, where x is the version number of pocketsphinx. The files should now be unarchived, and you can now build the code. Follow similar steps for these files, first `cd` to the `pocketSphinx` directory, then type `./configure` to see if you're ready to build the files. Then type `make`, wait for everything to build, then type `sudo make install`.

2.  Once you have completed the installation, you need to let the system know where your files are. To do this, edit the `/etc/ld.so.conf` file as root. Add the last line to the file, so it should now look like this:

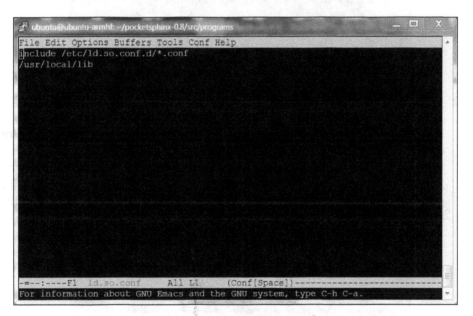

3.  Type `sudo /sbin/ldconfig` and the system will now be aware of your pocketsphinx libraries.

4. Once everything is installed, you can try your speech recognition. Change your directory to the `/home/ubuntu//pocketsphinx-0.8/src/programs` directory and try a demo program by typing `sudo ./pocketsphinx_continuous`. This program takes an input from the mic and turns it into a speech. After running the command, you'll get all kinds of information that won't have much meaning for you, and then get to this point:

5. Even though the warning message states that it can't find a mic or a capture element, it can find your mic element or a capture element. If you have set things up as previously described, you should be ready to give it a command. Say "hello" into the mic. When it senses that you have stopped speaking, it will process your speech, again giving us all kinds of interesting information that has no meaning for us, but should eventually showing this screen:

Notice the `000000001: hello` line. It recognized your speech! You can try other words and phrases. The system is very sensitive, so it might also pick up background noise. You are also going to find out that it is not very accurate. There are two ways to make it more accurate. One is to train the system to understand your voice more accurately. I'm not going to detail that process here. It's a bit complex, and if you want to know more, feel free to go to the CMU pocketsphinx website at `http://cmusphinx.sourceforge.net/`.

# Improving speech recognition accuracy

The second way to improve accuracy is to limit the number of words that your system can use to determine what you are saying. The default has literally thousands of words that are possible, so if two words are close, it might choose the wrong word as opposed to the word you spoke. In order to make the system more accurate, you are going to restrict the words it has to choose from. You can do this by making your own grammar.

The first step is to create a file with the words or phrases you want the system to recognize. Then you use a web tool to create two files that the system will use to define your grammar:

1. Create a file called `grammar.txt` and insert the following text in it:

2. Now you must use the CMU web browser tool to turn this file into two files that the system can use to define its dictionary. Open a web browser window and go to www.speech.cs.cmu.edu/tools/lmtool-new.html. If you click on the **Choose File** button, you can then find and select your file. It should look something like this:

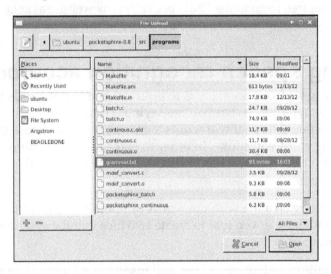

3. Open the grammer.txt file and on the web page, select **COMPILE KNOWLEDGE BASE**. The following window should pop up:

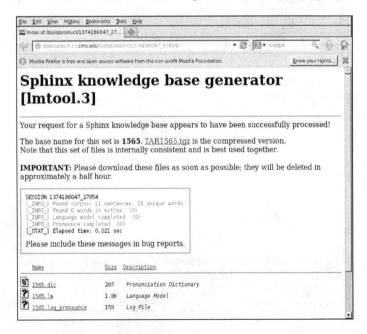

4. Now you need to download the `.tgz` file, that is, the tool created. In this case, it's the `TAR1565.tgz` file.

5. Move it to the `/home/ubuntu/pocketsphinx-0.8/src/programs` directory and unarchive it using `tar -xzvf` and the filename.

6. Now you can invoke the `pocketsphinx_continuous` program to use this dictionary by typing `sudo ./pocketsphinx_continuous -lm 1565.lm -dict 1565.dic`.

It will now look up that directory as it tries to find matches to your commands.

# Responding to voice commands

Now that your system can both hear and speak, you would want to provide the capability to respond to your speech, and perhaps even execute some commands based on the speech input. Now you're going to configure the system to respond to your simple commands.

In order to respond, you're going to edit the `continuous.c` code in the `/home/ubuntu/pocketsphinx-0.8/src/programs` directory. You can create your own `.c` file, but this file is already set up in the makefile system, and will serve as an excellent starting spot. You will need to edit the `continuous.c` file. It's very long, and a bit complicated, but you should be specifically looking out for the following section in the code:

```
File Edit Options Buffers Tools C Help
        while (ad_read(ad, adbuf, 4096) >= 0);
        cont_ad_reset(cont);

        printf("Stopped listening, please wait...\n");
        fflush(stdout);
        /* Finish decoding, obtain and print result */
        ps_end_utt(ps);
        hyp = ps_get_hyp(ps, NULL, &uttid);
        printf("%s: %s\n", uttid, hyp);
        fflush(stdout);

        /* Exit if the first word spoken was GOODBYE */
        if (hyp) {
            sscanf(hyp, "%s", word);
            if (strcmp(word, "goodbye") == 0)
                break;
        }

        /* Resume A/D recording for next utterance */
        if (ad_start_rec(ad) < 0)
            E_FATAL("Failed to start recording\n");
    }

    cont_ad_close(cont);
-=--:----F1  continuous.c    80% L327   (C/l Abbrev)----------------------
```

In this section of the code, the word has already been decoded, and is held in the `hyp` variable. You can add some code here to make your system do things based on the value associated with the word you have decoded. First, let's try adding the capability to respond to hello and goodbye, and see if you can get the program to stop. Make the following changes to the code:

```
File Edit Options Buffers Tools C Help
        fflush(stdout);
        /* Finish decoding, obtain and print result */
        ps_end_utt(ps);
        hyp = ps_get_hyp(ps, NULL, &uttid);
        printf("%s: %s\n", uttid, hyp);
        fflush(stdout);
        /* Exit if the first word spoken was GOODBYE */
        if (hyp) {
            sscanf(hyp, "%s", word);
            if (strcmp(hyp, "GOODBYE") == 0)
            {
                system("espeak \"good bye\"");
                break;
            }
            else if (strcmp(hyp, "HELLO") == 0)
            {
                system("espeak \"hello\"");
            }
        }

        /* Resume A/D recording for next utterance */
        if (ad_start_rec(ad) < 0)
            E_FATAL("Failed to start recording\n");
    }
-=--:----F1   continuous.c   79% L319    (C/l Abbrev)----------------------
```

Now you need to rebuild your code. Since the make system already knows how to build the `pocketsphinx_continuous` program, any time you make a change to the `continuous.c` file, it will rebuild the application. Simply type `make`. The file will compile and create a new version of `pocketsphinx_continuous`. To run your new version, type `sudo ./pocketsphinx_continuous`. Make sure you type `./` at the start of `pocketsphinx_continuous`. If you don't, the system has another version of `pocketsphinx_continuous` in the library and it will run that.

If everything is set correctly, saying hello should result in a response of hello from your BeagleBone Black. Saying goodbye should elicit a response of goodbye, as well as shutting down the program. Note that the system command can be used to actually run any program that you might run with a command line. You can now use this to have your program started and run other programs based on the voice commands.

# Adding additional hardware and software for a fully functional core system

The final step in making your BeagleBone Black really useful is to add a wireless LAN interface. This will allow you to control your robotic projects remotely without having a wired LAN cable. It is very straightforward, but there is one slight challenge. Adding a WLAN device might cause your BeagleBone Black to draw in more current than a USB power supply can provide, and your board will stop, that is, the blue light will no longer flash like a heartbeat.

To avoid this problem and provide additional capability to add more devices, you'll need to add a powered USB hub to your BeagleBone Black. This is a USB hub that is powered by an external power supply, not the BeagleBone.

Once you have this device connected to a power supply and to your BeagleBone Black, you can now connect your WLAN device. There are many different WLAN devices; you'll have to follow the instructions for your specific device. See `elinux.org/Beagleboard:BeagleBoneBlack`. Go to the **WIFI Adapters** section to see some devices that others have successfully used. I personally have had good luck with the Edimax device, and the instructions are very simple. To get this device connected, follow the instructions at `groups.google.com/forum/#!topic/beaglebone/Q92uD9F1us8`. Once you are connected via LAN, you can access the BeagleBone Black wirelessly via SSH and VNC viewer, controlling your robotic projects without limiting their movement.

# Summary

This chapter has been a bit long and a bit involving, but if you've followed everything, you should have a solid system that you can now use as the basis of your robotic projects. Your first project will be a fairly simple tracked robot. You'll add the speed and direction control, and then some sensing, and finally some commands and controls to make your device autonomous. So let's get building!

# 2
# Building a Basic Tracked Vehicle

Now you will add the capability to move the entire project using wheels. Perhaps the easiest way to make your project mobile is to use a vehicle with two tank tracks. In this chapter, you will be introduced to the basics of controlling DC motors and use the BeagleBone Black to control the speed and direction of your tracked platform.

In this chapter, you will be doing the following:

- Using a motor controller to control the speed of your tracked vehicle
- Controlling your mobile platform programmatically using the BeagleBone Black
- Using voice commands to control your tracked vehicle

## Choosing the tracked platform

The first step in building your mobile robot is to pick your tracked vehicle platform. There are several manufacturers that make preassembled, tracked units. Here's an image of a preassembled, inexpensive tracked platform, made by Dagu. It's called the **Dagu Rover 5 Tracked Chassis**.

Once you have chosen your mobile platform, you'll need to hook up a motor controller, a battery, and the BeagleBone Black.

# Connecting a motor controller to control the speed of your tracked platform

The first step to make the platform mobile is adding a motor controller. This allows us to control the speed of each wheel (or track) independently. Before you get started, let's spend some time understanding the basics of motor control. The unit moves by engaging the motors. If the desired direction is straight, the motors are run at the same speed. If you want to turn the unit, the motors are run at different speeds. The unit can turn in a circle if you run one motor forward and one backwards.

DC motors are fairly straightforward devices. The speed and direction of this motor are controlled by the magnitude and polarity of the voltage applied to its terminals. The higher the voltage, the faster the motor will turn. If you reverse the polarity of the voltage, you can reverse the direction in which the motor is turning.

The magnitude and polarity of the voltage are not the only important factors when you think about controlling the motors. The power that your motor can apply to move your platform is also determined by the voltage and the current supplied at its terminals.

There are GPIO pins on the BeagleBone Black. If you'd like to learn more about the specific capabilities of these pins, go to `http://beagleboard.org/Support/bone101`. In this project, you'll use them to create the control voltage and drive your motors. These pins provide direct access to some of the control lines available from the processor itself. However, the unit cannot source enough current, and your motors might not be able to generate enough power to move your mobile platform. You might also cause physical damage to your BeagleBone Black board. That is why you need to use the motor controller, as it will provide both voltage and current so that your platform can move reliably. In this case, I have chosen to hook up the motor controller via USB, making the connections and programming much simpler.

There are numerous possibilities for the motor controller. However, I'm going to suggest one that requires no internal programming and allows you to talk over USB to control the motors. You'll want one that can also control the two motors. The one I prefer is the Pololu TReX Jr Dual Motor Controller DMC02 from Pololu, orderable from `www.pololu.com` at `http://www.pololu.com/product/767`. Here is an image:

This piece of hardware will convert the USB commands to voltage that controls your motors.

# Choosing the battery

The first step in making your project mobile is connecting the motor controller to the platform. There are three connections you need to make:

- First, you need to connect a battery to the controller
- Second, you need to connect the motor controller to the motors themselves
- Third, you need to connect the motor controller to the BeagleBone Black

There are a couple of choices with respect to batteries. One choice is to use the battery holder that came with the platform. It should look like this:

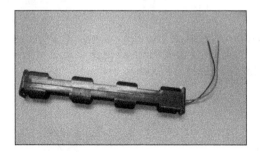

Another choice is to use a Li Po Poly RC battery; these carry a much longer charge. If you are going to do this, choose a 2S version, which is 2 cells in series. Here is an image of an RC battery, with connectors to make it easy to disconnect and charge:

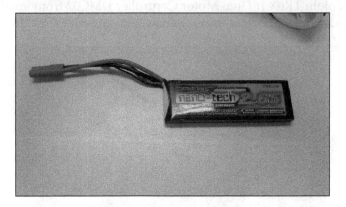

You'll also need a battery to power the BeagleBone Black. One easy choice is a cell phone battery that has a USB output. Here is an image of one such device:

This battery will provide more than enough power for your BeagleBone Black. If you chose one with two USB outputs, you'll be able to power a powered USB hub as well, which you will use later in this and in other projects.

# Connecting the motor controller

Once you've chosen your battery, you'll need to connect the motor controller to the battery and motor. Follow these steps:

1.  On the back of the motor controller, notice the labels **VIN**, **A M1 B**, **A M2 B**, and **GND**:

2.  Once you have the battery pack ready, insert the wires into the motor controller in the blue connectors marked **VIN** and **GND**. **VIN** is the constant DC voltage in from your batteries, and **GND** is the ground connection from your batteries. **A** and **B** are the control signals to your DC motors. You'll notice that on the battery connector, one of the wires is red. Insert it into the **VIN** connector, and then tighten the screw connector. On the battery connector, you'll notice that the other wire is black. Insert that wire into the connector marked **GND** and tighten the screw connector. The connections will look like this:

    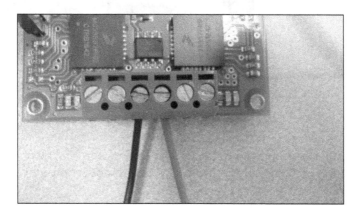

3.  Now connect one of the motors to the motor controller by connecting the red and black wires with male connectors to the two outer blue screw connectors, the red one to A and the black one to B using the male to male jumper wires. The connection to the motor controller should look like this:

After performing all the preceding steps, the connections to the motor should now look like this:

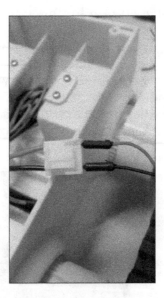

Now your controller is connected to the battery and motor. The next step is to make sure that the controller works, by connecting it to a remote computer.

Here I would insert a complete layout to connect/power the boards:

- USB hub
- BeagleBoard
- Might be the battery for BeagleBoard

# Connecting the motor controller system

You can now connect the DC motor controller to the USB cable. Here are the steps:

1. The motor controller is going to need a serial input, but you'll find it easiest to talk over USB. The USB-to-TTL serial cable is available at amazon.com and a number of other suppliers. Here is an image:

2. To do so, connect the TTL end of the cable to the serial connector on the board. On the underside of the board, you will see the following labels:

3.  Now connect the green cable to the SI connection, the white cable to the SO connection, and the black cable to the G connection. Here is an image of what it should look like:

4.  Now, there's one more step before you connect the board to the BeagleBone Black. Remove the jumper at the top of the board so that the board will accept serial commands. Here's an image of the jumper, and I like to just turn it sideways so that I don't lose the jumper:

You should supply the unit with power by making sure you have batteries in the battery holder. Now that you have your basic motor controller functionality up and running, you need to connect the motor controller to the BeagleBone Black. Plug the USB cable that you just connected to the motor controller to the BeagleBone Black.

Here is an image of all the pieces of hardware that you have connected:

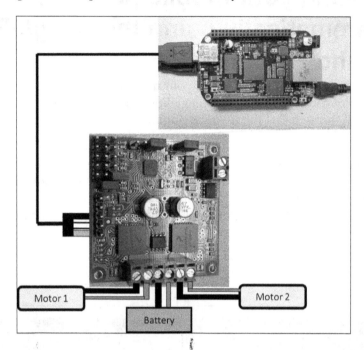

You might want to configure all of the hardware on top of the mobile platform like this:

Your platform is now assembled The next step will be to control this movement using the BeagleBone Black.

# Controlling your mobile platform programmatically using the BeagleBone Black and Python

Now that you have your motor running, your next step is to programmatically control the motor controller using the BeagleBone Black. If you are going to do this remotely, log in through PuTTY. If you are doing this directly on a monitor, simply log in.

I suggest you use Python in your initial attempts to control the motor. It is very straightforward to write, run, and debug your code in Python. I am going to include the directions here for Python; you can also go to the Pololu.com website at www.pololu.com/ and find instructions for how to access the capabilities in the C programming language.

The first Python program you are going to create is shown here:

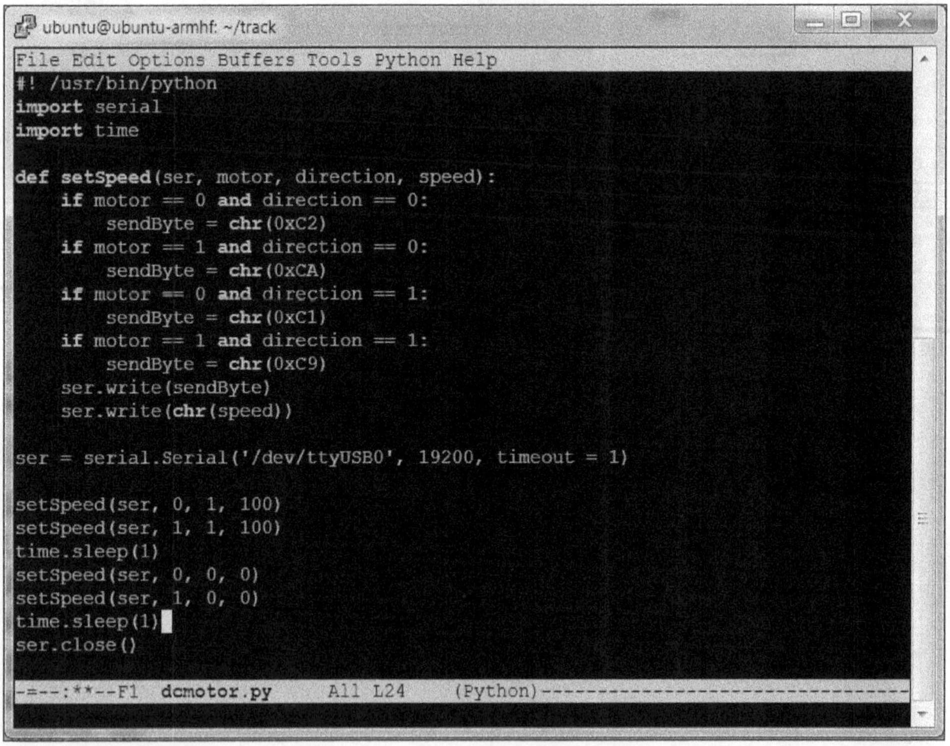

```
ubuntu@ubuntu-armhf: ~/track
File Edit Options Buffers Tools Python Help
#! /usr/bin/python
import serial
import time

def setSpeed(ser, motor, direction, speed):
    if motor == 0 and direction == 0:
        sendByte = chr(0xC2)
    if motor == 1 and direction == 0:
        sendByte = chr(0xCA)
    if motor == 0 and direction == 1:
        sendByte = chr(0xC1)
    if motor == 1 and direction == 1:
        sendByte = chr(0xC9)
    ser.write(sendByte)
    ser.write(chr(speed))

ser = serial.Serial('/dev/ttyUSB0', 19200, timeout = 1)

setSpeed(ser, 0, 1, 100)
setSpeed(ser, 1, 1, 100)
time.sleep(1)
setSpeed(ser, 0, 0, 0)
setSpeed(ser, 1, 0, 0)
time.sleep(1)
ser.close()

-=--:**--F1  dcmotor.py      All L24     (Python)--------------------------
```

To create this program, create a directory called `track` in your home directory by typing `mkdir track`, and then type `cd track`. You should now be in the `track` directory. Now open the file by typing `emacs dcmotor.py`. If you are using the nano editor, open a new file using `nano dcmotor.py`. Now enter the program. Let's go through the program:

- `#!/usr/bin/python`: The first line allows your program to be run outside of the Python environment. You'll use it later when you want to execute your code using voice commands.

- `import serial`: The next line imports the serial library. You need this to talk to your motor controllers. In order to run this program, you'll need the serial library. Install it by typing `sudo apt-get install python-serial` in the prompt. You'll then need to add yourself to the dialout group by typing `sudo adduser ubuntu dialout`. Then do a `sudo reboot` to enable all these changes.

- `import time`: This line imports the time library, you'll need this to add some delays in your code. You don't have to download this library, it's available with the standard Python programming framework.

- `def setSpeed(ser, motor, direction, speed)`: This function sets the speed and direction of one of your two motors. Since you are going to control the motors throughout your program, it is easier if you put this functionality in a function:

  ```
  if motor == 0 and direction == 0:
  ```

- `sendByte = chr(0xC2)`: This sets the address if you are going to send data to motor 1 in the forward direction. The hexadecimal characters are base 16 values that send specific bit patterns to the controller to set it to specific modes. See the documentation at `http://www.pololu.com/file/0J12/TReXJr_Commands_v1.2.pdf` for specifics on the commands accepted by the motor controller:

  ```
  if motor == 1 and direction == 0:
  ```

- `sendByte = chr(0xCA)`: This sets the address if you want to send data to motor 2 in the forward direction:

  ```
  if motor == 0 and direction == 1:
  ```

- `sendByte = chr(0xC1)`: This sets the address if you want to send data to motor 1 in the reverse direction:

  ```
  if motor == 0 and direction == 1:
  ```

- `sendByte = chr(0xC9)`: This sets the address if you are going to send data to motor 2 in the reverse direction.

- `ser.write(sendByte)`: This writes `sendByte` to the motor controller, which sets which motor moves and in which direction.

- `ser.write(chr(speed))`: This writes the speed to the motor controller, setting the speed.

- `ser = serial.Serial('/dev/ttyUSB0'ttyUSB0', 19200, timeout = 1)`: This opens a serial port. The name of this serial port depends on the type of cable you connect to the device, and other devices that might be connected. In this case, you are connected through the USB port and have only one device connected, so it will be named `ttyUSB0`.

- `setSpeed(ser, 0, 1, 100)`: This calls the function and sets the speed of the motor from 1 to 100.

- `setSpeed(ser, 1, 1, 100)`: This calls the function and sets the speed of the motor from 2 to 100. Note that you have to have this motor go in the opposite direction if you want the platform to move forward.

- `time.sleep(1)`: This allows the motor to wait for 1 second.

- `setSpeed(ser, 0, 0, 0)`: This calls the function and sets the speed of the motor from 1 to 0.

- `setSpeed(ser, 1, 0, 0)`: This calls the function and sets the speed of the motor from 2 to 0.

- `time.sleep(1)`: This allows the motor to wait for 1 second.

- `ser.close()`: This closes the serial port.

**Downloading the example code**

You can download the example code files for all Packt books you have purchased from your account at `http://www.packtpub.com`. If you purchased this book elsewhere, you can visit `http://www.packtpub.com/support` and register to have the files e-mailed directly to you.

With this installed, you can run your program. To do this, type `python dcmotor.py`. Your motor should run for 1 second and then stop. You can now control the motor through Python! Additionally, you'll want to make this program available to run from the command line. Type `chmod +x dcmotor.py`. If you now type `ls`, that is, list all programs, you'll see that your program is now green, which means you can execute it directly. Now you can type `./dcmotor.py`.

Now that you know the basics of commanding your mobile platform, feel free to add even more `setSpeed` commands to make your mobile platform move. Running just one motor will make the platform turn, as will running both motors in opposite directions.

# Adding program arguments to control your platform

Let's also add the capability to send the program arguments, including which motors you want to run and for how long. Then you'll be able to call this program from other programs.

You'll make two modifications to the program. This first will look like this:

```
ubuntu@ubuntu-armhf:~/track
File Edit Options Buffers Tools Python Help
#! /usr/bin/python
import serial
import time
import sys

def setSpeed(ser, motor, direction, speed):
    if motor == 0 and direction == 0:
        sendByte = chr(0xC2)
    if motor == 1 and direction == 0:
        sendByte = chr(0xCA)
    if motor == 0 and direction == 1:
        sendByte = chr(0xC1)
    if motor == 1 and direction == 1:
        sendByte = chr(0xC9)
    ser.write(sendByte)
    ser.write(chr(speed))

ser = serial.Serial('/dev/ttyUSB0', 19200, timeout = 1)
if int(sys.argv[1]) == 1:
    setSpeed(ser, 0, 1, 100)
    setSpeed(ser, 1, 1, 100)
    time.sleep(float(sys.argv[2]))
    setSpeed(ser, 0, 0, 0)
    setSpeed(ser, 1, 0, 0)
if int(sys.argv[1]) == 2:
-=--:----F1   dcmotor.py      Top L1      (Python)----------------------
```

In the top section, you'll add `import sys`. This brings in a library so that you can access the arguments when you actually execute your program. The main changes are in the body of the program. It will now look like this:

```
               sendByte = chr(0xCA)
        if motor == 0 and direction == 1:
               sendByte = chr(0xC1)
        if motor == 1 and direction == 1:
               sendByte = chr(0xC9)
        ser.write(sendByte)
        ser.write(chr(speed))

ser = serial.Serial('/dev/ttyUSB0', 19200, timeout = 1)
if int(sys.argv[1]) == 1:
        setSpeed(ser, 0, 1, 100)
        setSpeed(ser, 1, 1, 100)
        time.sleep(float(sys.argv[2]))
        setSpeed(ser, 0, 0, 0)
        setSpeed(ser, 1, 0, 0)
if int(sys.argv[1]) == 2:
        setSpeed(ser, 0, 0, 100)
        setSpeed(ser, 1, 0, 100)
        time.sleep(float(sys.argv[2]))
        setSpeed(ser, 0, 0, 0)
        setSpeed(ser, 1, 0, 0)
if int(sys.argv[1]) == 3:
        setSpeed(ser, 0, 0, 100)
        setSpeed(ser, 1, 1, 100)
        time.sleep(float(sys.argv[2]))
        setSpeed(ser, 0, 0, 0)
        setSpeed(ser, 1, 0, 0)
if int(sys.argv[1]) == 4:
        setSpeed(ser, 0, 1, 100)
        setSpeed(ser, 1, 0, 100)
        time.sleep(float(sys.argv[2]))
        setSpeed(ser, 0, 0, 0)
        setSpeed(ser, 1, 0, 0)
if int(sys.argv[1]) == 5:
        setSpeed(ser, 0, 0, 0)
        setSpeed(ser, 1, 0, 0)
ser.close()
```

The addition is the `if int(sys.argv[1]) == 1` and subsequent clauses. The program checks the value of `sys.argv[1]`, or the first argument given to it. In this case, you'll use two arguments. The first will tell the program which motors to run and in which direction (1 for forward, 2 for backward, 3 for turn right, and 4 for turn left) and the second will tell the program how long to run the motor.

Now when you run the program, you'll want to include two numbers when you call the program. For example, if you want the unit to go forward for 1 second, type `./dcmotor.py 1 1`. If you want the unit to turn right for 2 seconds, type `./dcmotor.py 3 2`.

# Accessing motor control via voice commands

You can now run this program from your remote computer using SSH and your unit will execute your command. But it would also be interesting to add voice control to your tracked project, so that you can give it voice commands and it will respond. To do this, you'll add some code to the pocketsphinx code that you installed in *Chapter 1, Preparing the BeagleBone Black*.

You'll first want to follow the directions from the previous chapter to create a dictionary with the commands for your robot. Here's an example of a text file dictionary for your robot:

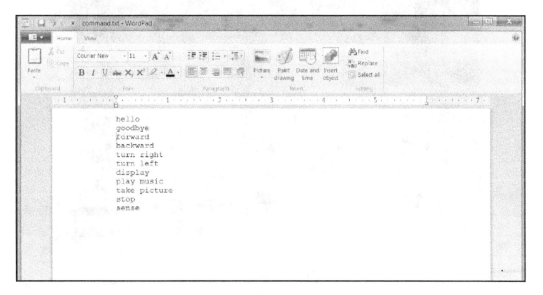

You'll also need to modify your voice recognition program so that it will run your Python program when it gets a voice command. You are going to make a simple modification to the `continuous.c` program in `/home/ubuntu/pocketsphinx-0.8/src/programs`. To do this, type `cd /home/ubuntu/ pocketsphinx-0.8/src/programs` and then type `emacs continuous.c`. The changes will come in the same section as your other voice commands, and will look like this:

```
ubuntu@ubuntu-armhf: ~/pocketsphinx-0.8/src/programs
File Edit Options Buffers Tools C Help
        hyp = ps_get_hyp(ps, NULL, &uttid);
        printf("%s: %s\n", uttid, hyp);
        fflush(stdout);

        /* Exit if the first word spoken was GOODBYE */
        if (hyp) {
            sscanf(hyp, "%s", word);
            if (strcmp(word, "GOODBYE") == 0)
                {
                    system("espeak \"good bye\"");
                    break;
                }
            if (strcmp(hyp, "HELLO") == 0)
                {
                    system("espeak \"hello\"");
                }
            if (strcmp(hyp, "FORWARD") == 0)
                {
                    system("espeak \"moving robot\"");
                    system("/home/ubuntu/track/dcmotor.py 1 1 ");
                }

        }

        /* Resume A/D recording for next utterance */
        if (ad_start_rec(ad) < 0)
            E_FATAL("Failed to start recording\n");
    }

    cont_ad_close(cont);
    ad_close(ad);
}
-=--:----F1  continuous.c   79% L338   (C/l Abbrev)-----------------------------
```

The additions are pretty straightforward. Let's walk through them:

- `else if (strcmp(hyp, "FORWARD") == 0)`: This checks the word as recognized by your voice command program. If it corresponds with the word FORWARD, it will execute everything inside the `if` statement. You use `{ }` to group and tell the system which commands go with this `else if` clause.

- `system("espeak \"moving robot\"")`: This executes `espeak`, which should tell you that you are about to run your robot program. By the way, you need to type `\"` because the `"` character is a special character in Linux, and if you want the actual `"` character, you need to precede it with the `\` character.

- `system("/home/ubuntu/track/dcmotor.py 1 1 ")`: This is the program you will execute. In this case, your mobile platform will do whatever the `dcmotor.py` program tells it to do with the two arguments. In this case, you will move forward for 1 second.

After doing this, you will need to recompile the program, so type `make` and the `pocketsphinx_continuous` executable will be created. Run the program by typing `sudo ./pocketsphinx_continuous -lm YourDict.lm -dict YourDict.dic` where `YourDict` is replaced by the number the pocketsphinx process created when you created your dictionary. Disconnect the LAN cable, and the mobile platform will now take the forward voice command and execute your program.

You can then add the additional commands to go backwards, to turn right or left, and to stop, as shown here:

```
ubuntu@ubuntu-armhf: ~/pocketsphinx-0.8/src/programs
File Edit Options Buffers Tools C Help

        /* Exit if the first word spoken was GOODBYE */
        if (hyp) {
            sscanf(hyp, "%s", word);
            if (strcmp(word, "GOODBYE") == 0)
                {
                    system("espeak \"good bye\"");
                    break;
                }
            if (strcmp(hyp, "HELLO") == 0)
                {
                    system("espeak \"hello\"");
                }
            if (strcmp(hyp, "FORWARD") == 0)
                {
                    system("espeak \"robot forward\"");
                    system("/home/ubuntu/track/dcmotor.py 1 5 ");
                }
            if (strcmp(hyp, "BACKWARD") == 0)
                {
                    system("espeak \"robot backward\"");
                    system("/home/ubuntu/track/dcmotor.py 2 5 ");
                }
            if (strcmp(hyp, "TURN RIGHT") == 0)
                {
                    system("espeak \"robot turn right\"");
                    system("/home/ubuntu/track/dcmotor.py 3 1 ");
                }
            if (strcmp(hyp, "TURN LEFT") == 0)
                {
                    system("espeak \"robot turn left\"");
                    system("/home/ubuntu/track/dcmotor.py 4 1 ");
                }
            if (strcmp(hyp, "STOP") == 0)
                {
                    system("espeak \"stopping robot\"");
                    system("/home/ubuntu/track/dcmotor.py 5 1 ");
                }
-=--:----F1  continuous.c   75% L344   (C/l Abbrev)-------------------------
```

You now have a complete mobile platform! When you execute your program, the mobile platform can now move around according to what you have programmed it to do. You can adjust the time settings so that your right and left turns are precise, and you can run forward or backward as long as you like.

## Summary

Now you have a basic tracked, mobile platform. You can control the unit remotely or give it voice commands. In the next chapter, you'll add some sonar and IR sensors so that you can avoid or track objects. This will allow your tracked vehicle to move around without hitting barriers.

# 3

# Adding Sensors to Your Tracked Vehicle

Now that your platform can move around, you'd want to add some sensors to avoid or track barriers or other objects. Sensors can also tell you the direction in which you are going. Adding sensors will give a sense of direction and intelligence to your robot.

In this chapter, you will learn the following:

- Using sonar sensors to find the distance to an object
- Using **Infrared (IR)** sensors to find distance to an object
- Some basic path planning techniques for your robot

## Basics of sensors

There are many different kinds of sensors. There are sensors that measure distance, temperature, wind strength, and direction. The list is almost endless. In almost every case, the sensor will take some sort of measurement and then turn it into a voltage that the BeagleBone Black can measure and programmatically respond to. There are many different interfaces for these measurement devices; over the next few chapters, you'll explore many of them. But to start, you'll learn how to measure distance using sonar and IR sensors.

## Adding distance sensors

If your robot is to appear intelligent, gathering information about the world around it will be crucial. So, let's add some sensors that can provide you information about the distance and location of barriers.

There are basically two kinds of distance sensors, **IR** and **sonar** sensors. Both send out a signal and then measure a response to calculate the distance of the object from themselves. You can use either sensor, so you'll learn how to add both to your project. Let's cover sonar sensors first.

# Sonar sensors

A sonar sensor uses ultrasonic sound to calculate the distance of an object. The sound wave travels out from the sensor, as illustrated here:

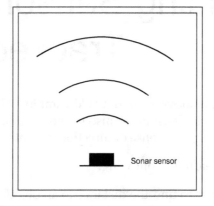

The device sends out a sound wave 10 times a second. If an object is in the path of these waves, then the waves reflect off the object, sending waves that return to the sensor, as shown here:

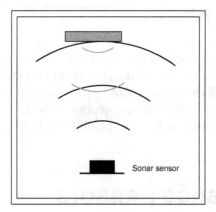

The sensor then measures return of waves, if any. It then uses the time difference between when the sound wave was sent out and when it returns to measure the distance to the object.

There are several types of sonar sensors, including some that connect directly to the BeagleBone Black using a USB port. The following is an image of this type of sensor, the USB-ProxSonar-EZ, available at `www.maxbotix.com/Ultrasonic_Sensors.htm#HRUSB-EZ`:

# Adding an array of inexpensive sonar sensors to the project

The sensor is quite easy to add but a bit expensive. In this project, you'll want to use three sensors, one to sense what is in front of your robot, and one on each corner so that you can decide which direction to turn to avoid the obstacle. In order to do this without adding significantly more hardware, you have to build an array of three inexpensive sensors. Here is an image of an inexpensive sonar sensor available at most of the online electronics outlets:

This particular sensor does not have a USB interface but only four pins, one each for **5V**, **GND**, **Trig** which sends a sonar pulse, and echo which receives the sonar pulse. One alternative is to connect your sensors to the BeagleBone Black since it has GPIO pins.

There are two issues with connecting this device directly to the BeagleBone Black:

• The first is that the device wants to send and receive 5-volt signals, but the BeagleBone Black does not want to send and receive 5-volt signals. Rather, a signal that is no larger than 3.3 volts. This can be solved by using a level shifter. This does add more hardware however. You can buy these types of level shifters from places such as `adafruit.com`. Here is an image of a level shifter:

The website at `www.adafruit.com` shows you how to use these level shifters to communicate with devices that require 5 V. Here is a link for the details from Adafruit:

`https://www.adafruit.com/products/1875`

• The second issue — one that is a bit more difficult to solve — is the non-real-time nature of the Linux operating system that runs on the BeagleBone Black. This particular issue requires that you send an output signal, and then calculate the time difference between this output signal and another input signal. In theory, this works fine. However, Linux does not provide real-time control. That means that if the system is busy doing something else, this time can be incorrect or is not reported at all. This is particularly true if the BeagleBone is off doing something processor intensive, such as video processing.

To solve these problems in a fairly inexpensive and reliable fashion, you're going to use an Arduino, and inexpensive real-time processor, to get the data and then communicate it to the BeagleBone Black.

For a much more advanced solution, you can use the BeagleBone Black **Programmable Real-time Unit** (PRU) and control the sensor. For information on this solution, see http://hackaday.com/2014/06/22/an-introduction-to-the-beaglebone-pru/ or http://www.element14.com/community/community/designcenter/single-board-computers/next-gen_beaglebone/blog/2013/05/22/bbb--working-with-the-pru-icssprussv2.

To sense distance, you'll use an Arduino to capture the data and its USB port to communicate the data to the BeagleBone Black. For instructions on how to interface the Arduino with the sonar sensor, see https://code.google.com/p/arduino-new-ping/ or http://www.instructables.com/id/Ultrasonic-Range-detector-using-Arduino-and-the-SR/. The Arduino will output the sensor data to the USB port. Connect the Arduino to the BeagleBone Black via the USB port. Create a Python program on the BeagleBone Black that can read the values. The code will look like this:

```
#!/usr/bin/python
import serial
import time

ser = serial.Serial('/dev/ttyACM0', 115200, timeout = 1)
while 1:
    x = ser.read(24)
    print (x)
    time.sleep(1)
```

You can use three sensors, one for the front of the tracked vehicle, and one for each side, and interface them all with the same Arduino. When you run the program with the sonar sensor, you'll see the three readings like this:

```
ubuntu@ubuntu-armhf: ~/track
0=5cm  1=154cm  2=127cm
0=5cm  1=155cm  2=126cm
0=5cm  1=154cm  2=126cm
0=5cm  1=154cm  2=126cm
0=5cm  1=154cm  2=127cm
0=5cm  1=154cm  2=126cm
0=5cm  1=154cm  2=126cm
0=5cm  1=153cm  2=126cm
0=5cm  1=154cm  2=126cm
0=5cm  1=154cm  2=126cm
0=5cm  1=154cm  2=127cm
0=5cm  1=155cm  2=126cm
```

Now you can use the sonar sensors to detect objects both in front and on each side of your robot.

# IR sensors

Another type of sensor that can make your project sense objects is the IR sensor. In this section, you'll learn the basics of IR sensing using the BeagleBone Black. First, let's have a little tutorial on IR sensors. The sensor you will be using will have a transmitter and a receiver. The transmitter part of the sensor sends a narrow beam of light, and the receiver part receives this beam of light. The difference in transit ends up as an angle measurement at the sensor, as shown here:

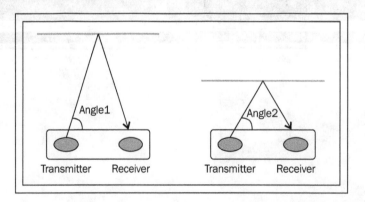

The different angles give you an indication of the distance to the object. Unfortunately, the relationship between the output of the sensor and the distance is not linear, so you'll need to do some calibration to predict the actual distance and its relationship to the output of the sensor. You'll learn more on that later.

There are several IR sensors that you can use to connect to the BeagleBone Black. A common sensor is the sharp IR sensor, and it comes in several different distance specifications. Here is an image of the 20 x 150 cm version:

There are two ways to connect the IR sensor to the BeagleBone Black. The first is to use a USB interface designed to connect the IR sensor to any standard USB interface, for example, the one from `phidgets.com`. This board is really amazing. It takes the analog signals, turns them into digital signals, and then makes them available so that they can be read from the USB port. The model number of this board is 1011_0 - PhidgetInterfaceKit 2/2/2 and its details can be found at `http://www.phidgets.com/products.php?category=0&product_id=1011_0`. Here is an image:

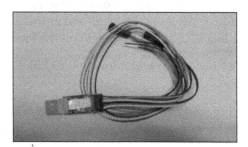

The details for connecting this can be found on the `www.phidgets.com` website.

You can also connect this sensor to the BeagleBone Black and use the BeagleBone Black's internal A/D converter. You won't have the real-time constraints of the sonar sensor, so finding the distance can be as easy as reading the voltage from the device and then translating it to a distance. The sensor will need **5V** and **GND** from the BeagleBone Black, and will supply an analog input between 0 and 5 volts that indicates the distance.

The BeagleBone Black cannot take in this analog input directly, as the maximum voltage it can handle is 1.8 volts. So you'll need to add a level shifter like the one shown earlier in this chapter. You'll connect the output of the sensor to one side of the level shifter, and the output of the other side of the level shifter will go to the GPIO pins on the BeagleBone Black. There are two expansion connectors on the BeagleBone Black, one on each side of the board. They are labeled P8 and P9. Here is an image with the pinout:

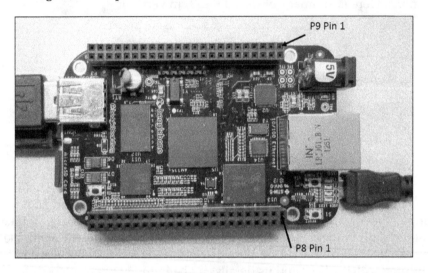

Connect the 5V of the sensor to the P9_3 on the BeagleBone Black, and the **GND** to P9_1 on the BeagleBone Black. Connect the **Vo** on the sensor to the **hv** side of your level shifter, and the **lv** side of the level shifter to one of the ADC inputs, for example, P9_39 on the BeagleBone Black. Connect the **GND** on the level shifter to P9_2.

Now you'll need to add a library that will allow you to talk to the GPIO pins via Python. Follow these steps:

1. Install the following packages: `sudo apt-get install build-essential python-dev python-setuptools python-pip python-smbus -y`

2. Type the following: `sudo easy_install -U distribute`

3. Now type `sudo pip install Adafruit_BBIO`. This will install the Adafruit library for talking via the GPIO pins.

4. To test your installation, type `sudo python -c "import Adafruit_BBIO.GPIO as GPIO; print GPIO"`. You should see this:

```
ubuntu@ubuntu-armhf:~$ sudo python -c "import Adafruit_BBIO.GPIO as GPIO; print
GPIO"
[sudo] password for ubuntu:
<module 'Adafruit_BBIO.GPIO' from '/usr/local/lib/python2.7/dist-packages/Adafru
it_BBIO/GPIO.so'>
ubuntu@ubuntu-armhf:~$
```

Now you are ready to write some Python code to read the ADC input. Here is the code:

```python
#!/usr/bin/python

# Import required Python libraries
import time
import Adafruit_BBIO.ADC as ADC
ADC.setup()
ADC_INPUT = "P9_39"

print "IR Measurement"

while 1:
# Allow module to settle
  time.sleep(0.5)

  value = ADC.read(ADC_INPUT)
  voltage = value * 1.8
  print(value)
```

```
-=--:----F1  irsensor.py    All L8    (Python)-----------------------------
Wrote /home/ubuntu/track/irsensor.py
```

And here is a sample output when the program is executed. When you run this program, you'll need to type `sudo python irsensor.py`.

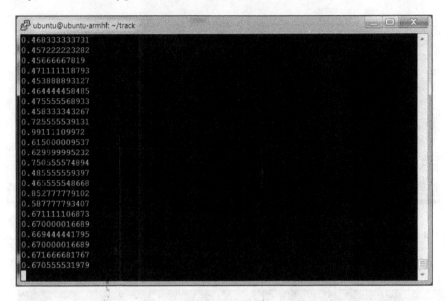

```
ubuntu@ubuntu-armhf: ~/track
0.468333333731
0.457222223282
0.45666667819
0.471111118793
0.453888893127
0.464444458485
0.475555568933
0.458333343267
0.725555539131
0.99111109972
0.615000009537
0.629999995232
0.750555574894
0.485555559397
0.465555548668
0.852777779102
0.587777793407
0.671111106873
0.670000016689
0.669444441795
0.670000016689
0.671666681767
0.670555531979
```

You'll notice that the values are returned in voltages; you can use this voltage as a trigger. When a certain voltage is reached, you can sense that you are close to a barrier. You can also turn the voltage into distance, although this is difficult as the sensor is not linear. See `davstott.me.uk/index.php/2013/06/02/raspberry-pi-sharp-infrared/` for a tutorial on turning the output of the sensor to an equation that you can use to find the distance using the voltage out from the sensor. You can easily see that adding two more IR sensors will create a three sensor array, much like you did in the *Sonar sensors* section.

Now that you have sensors, you can use them to avoid obstacles and do route planning.

# Dynamic path planning for your robot

Now that you can see barriers, you'll want to do dynamic path planning. Dynamic path planning simply means that you don't have knowledge of the entire world with all the possible barriers before you encounter them. This can be a complex topic, but there are some basics that you can start to understand and apply as you ask your robot to move around its environment. Let's start with the idea of planning a path without barriers, and then add barriers.

# Basic path planning

In order to talk about dynamic path planning, you'll need a framework to both understand where your robot is and determine the location of the goal. The most commonly used framework is an *x-y* grid. Here is a diagram of such a grid:

There are three key locations or points in the grid:

- The first point is a fixed reference position. All other positions will be measured with respect to this position.

- The second point is the location of your robot. Your robot will keep track of its location using its *x* coordinate, or position with respect to some fixed reference position in the *x* direction; and its *y* coordinate, or its position with respect to some fixed reference position in the *y* direction to the goal. When you first place your robot on the grid, you must place it facing a known direction, for example, the front facing the positive *x* direction, so that you can calculate how to turn your robot to the desired angle.

- The third point is the position of the goal, also given in *x* and *y* coordinates with respect to the fixed reference position. If you know these three points and the starting angle of your robot, you can plan an optimum—or shortest distance—path to the goal. To do this, you can use the goal location and the robot location and some fairly simple math to calculate the distance and angle from the robot to the goal.

To calculate the distance, use the following equation:

$$d = \sqrt{\left( \left( X\,goal - X\,goal \right)^2 + \left( Y\,goal - Y\,robot \right)^2 \right)}$$

You'll use this equation to tell your robot how far to travel to the goal. A second equation will tell your robot the angle it needs to travel:

$$\theta = \arctan\left( \frac{Y\,goal - Y\,robot}{X\,goal - X\,robot} \right)$$

Here is a graphical representation of these two pieces of information:

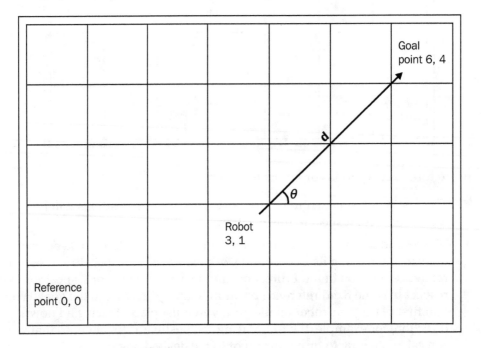

Now that you have the goal angle and distance, you can program your robot to move. To do this, you will write a program to do path planning, and access the `dcmotor.py` program you wrote in *Chapter 2, Building a Basic Tracked Vehicle*. However, you will need to know the distance that your robot travels in a given length of time so that you can tell your robot how far to travel using time units instead of distance units. The best way to do this is to run the `dcmotor.py` program for 1 second and measure the distance. This will be a scaling factor you can use to translate between the distances that you calculate with your path planning program and the arguments that you will send to your `dcmotor.py` program.

You'll also need to be able to translate the seconds that you command your robot to run in the `dcmotor.py` program to the change in the angle that will occur in degrees/seconds. With these two pieces of information, you can move your robot to the goal.

You can also use a gyroscope and an accelerometer for your project to measure the actual distance and direction. As with the sonar sensor, the easiest way to do this is to interface the device directly to an Arduino and then use a USB connection to read the values to the BeagleBone Black. See `http://www.instructables.com/id/Use-an-Accelerometer-and-Gyroscope-with-Arduino/` for more details. For instructions on how to connect the accelerometer directly to the BeagleBone Black, see `http://beagleboard.org/Support/BoneScript/accelerometer/`.

Here are the steps you will perform:

1. Calculate the distance in units that your robot will need to travel to reach the goal. Convert this to seconds that your motors will run to achieve this distance.

2. Calculate the angle that your robot will need to travel to reach the goal. Convert this in both a turn direction and seconds that your motors will need to run to achieve this angle.

3. Call the `dcmotor.py` program with the proper direction and seconds argument to move your robot to the correct angle.

4. Call the `dcmotor.py` program with the proper direction and seconds argument to move your robot to the correct distance. Note that you can choose between moving your robot in the forward direction or backward direction, which will change your angle setting calculated previously by 180 degrees.

That's it! Here is some Python code that executes the preceding steps. The user enters the robot's current location, starting angle, and goal location, and the robot moves to the goal.

```
ubuntu@ubuntu-armhf: ~/track
File Edit Options Buffers Tools Python Help
#! /usr/bin/python
import math
import time
import os

xpos_robot = int(raw_input("Robot X Position: "))
ypos_robot = int(raw_input("Robot Y Position: "))
xpos_goal = int(raw_input("Goal X Position: "))
ypos_goal = int(raw_input("Goal Y Position: "))

distance = math.sqrt((xpos_goal - xpos_robot)**2 + (ypos_goal - ypos_robot)**2)
angle = round(math.degrees(math.atan2((ypos_goal - ypos_robot), (xpos_goal - xp\
os_robot))))
if angle<0:
    angle += 360
print distance, angle
angle = (angle / 100)   # convert degress to time running
# Move angle first
os.system("python dcmotor.py 3 " + str(angle))
time.sleep(2)
# Now move distance
os.system("python dcmotor.py 1 " + str(distance))
-=--:**--F1   path.py      All L18    (Python)----------------------------
Auto-saving...done
```

# Avoiding obstacles

Planning paths without obstacles is, as has been shown, quite easy. However, it becomes a bit more challenging when your robot needs to avoid obstacles. Let's look at the case where there is an obstacle in the path you calculated previously. It might look like this:

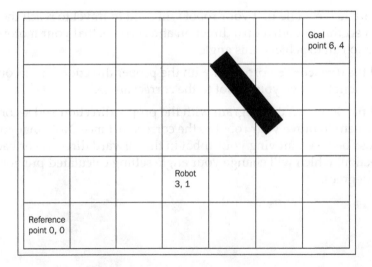

You can use the same path planning algorithm to find the starting angle. However, you'll now need to use your sonar sensors to detect the obstacle. When your sonar sensors detect the obstacle, you'll need to stop and recalculate the desired path. Now you can look down on the problem and see that in this case, the robot should turn right by 90 degrees, go until the obstacle ends, and then recalculate the optimum path. However, your robot cannot know how big the obstacle is, so it will need a way to navigate in the presence of an obstacle of unknown size and position.

There are a lot of different possibilities, but in order to keep your robot simple, let's have your robot turn to the right by 90 degrees when it encounters an obstacle, and move forward till a given distance. This will move the robot to a new $x$ and $y$ location. Then have the robot recalculate the optimum path to the goal based on the new robot $x$ and $y$ locations, and then have it try to move to the goal using the new angle and distance. If it encounters another obstacle, it will repeat the process until it reaches the goal. In this case, using these rules, the robot will travel the following path:

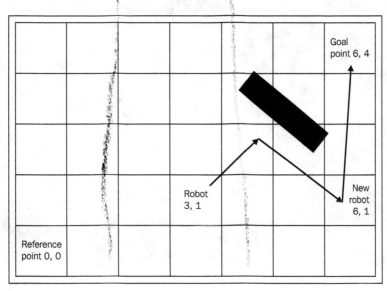

And here is the first part of the Python code when utilizing only the front sonar sensor on the sonar sensor array:

```
ubuntu@ubuntu-armhf: ~/track
File Edit Options Buffers Tools Python Help
#! /usr/bin/python
import math
import time
import os
import serial

def calcDistance(xpos_goal, ypos_goal, xpos_robot, ypos_robot):
    distance = math.sqrt((xpos_goal - xpos_robot)**2 + (ypos_goal - ypos_robot)**2)
    return distance

def calcAngle(xpos_goal, ypos_goal, xpos_robot, ypos_robot):
    angle = round(math.degrees(math.atan2((ypos_goal - ypos_robot), (xpos_goal - xpos_robo\
t))))
    if angle > 180:
        angle -= 360
    if angle < -180:
        angle += 360
    return angle

def moveRobot(distance, angle):
    angle = (angle / 95)    # convert degress to time running
    if angle > 0:
        os.system("python dcmotor.py 3 " + str(angle))
    else:
        angle = abs(angle)
        os.system("python dcmotor.py 4 " + str(angle))
    time.sleep(2)
    os.system("python dcmotor.py 1 " + str(distance) + "&")
    return

def findRange(x):
    pos1 = x.find("1=")
    pos2 = x.find("cm",pos1 + 2)
    if pos1 > 0 and pos2 > 0:
        range = int(x[pos1 + 2:pos2])
    else:
        range = 0
    return range

ser = serial.Serial('/dev/ttyACM0', 115200, timeout = 1)
xpos_robot = int(raw_input("Robot X Position: "))
ypos_robot = int(raw_input("Robot Y Position: "))
xpos_goal = int(raw_input("Goal X Position: "))
ypos_goal = int(raw_input("Goal Y Position: "))
-=--:**--F1  obstacle.py    Top L1     (Python)----------------------------------
```

The second part of the Python code is shown in the following screenshot:

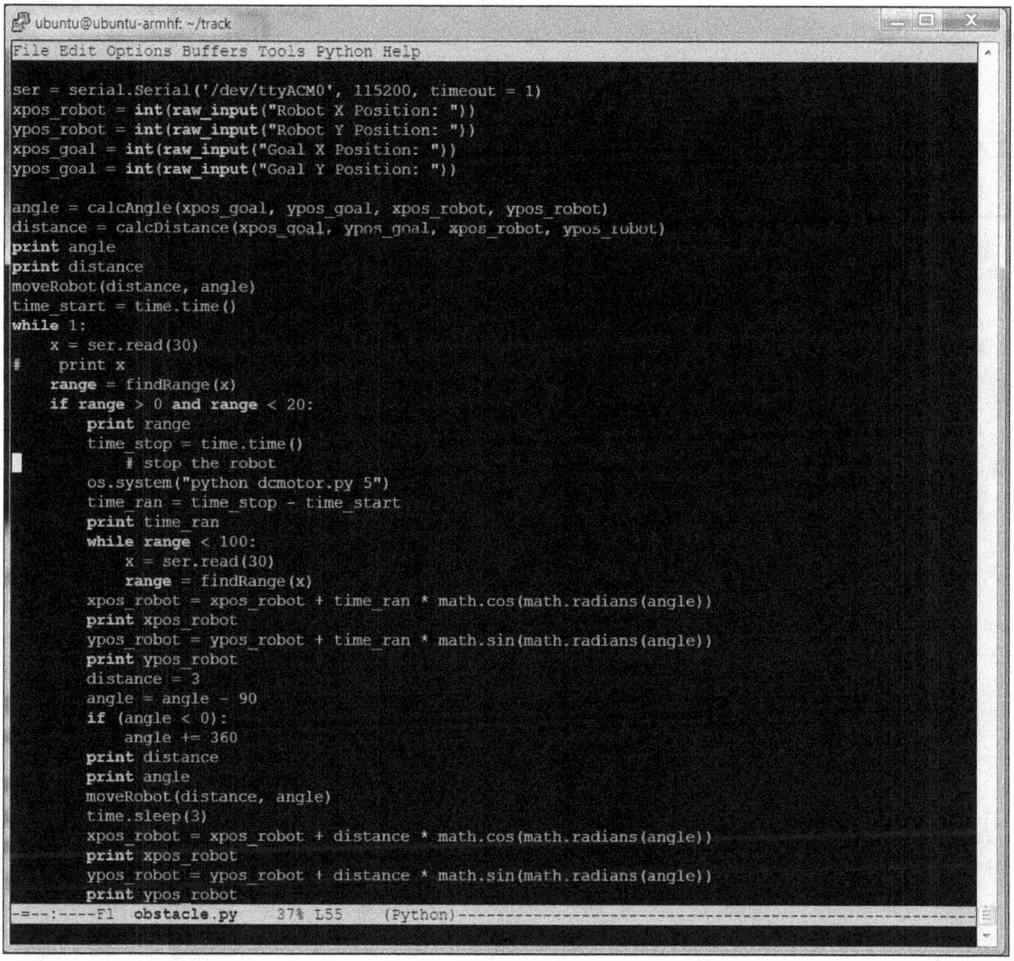

```
ubuntu@ubuntu-armhf: ~/track
File Edit Options Buffers Tools Python Help
ser = serial.Serial('/dev/ttyACM0', 115200, timeout = 1)
xpos_robot = int(raw_input("Robot X Position: "))
ypos_robot = int(raw_input("Robot Y Position: "))
xpos_goal = int(raw_input("Goal X Position: "))
ypos_goal = int(raw_input("Goal Y Position: "))

angle = calcAngle(xpos_goal, ypos_goal, xpos_robot, ypos_robot)
distance = calcDistance(xpos_goal, ypos_goal, xpos_robot, ypos_robot)
print angle
print distance
moveRobot(distance, angle)
time_start = time.time()
while 1:
    x = ser.read(30)
#    print x
    range = findRange(x)
    if range > 0 and range < 20:
        print range
        time_stop = time.time()
            # stop the robot
        os.system("python dcmotor.py 5")
        time_ran = time_stop - time_start
        print time_ran
        while range < 100:
            x = ser.read(30)
            range = findRange(x)
        xpos_robot = xpos_robot + time_ran * math.cos(math.radians(angle))
        print xpos_robot
        ypos_robot = ypos_robot + time_ran * math.sin(math.radians(angle))
        print ypos_robot
        distance = 3
        angle = angle - 90
        if (angle < 0):
            angle += 360
        print distance
        print angle
        moveRobot(distance, angle)
        time.sleep(3)
        xpos_robot = xpos_robot + distance * math.cos(math.radians(angle))
        print xpos_robot
        ypos_robot = ypos_robot + distance * math.sin(math.radians(angle))
        print ypos_robot
-=--:----F1  obstacle.py    37% L55    (Python)---------------------------------
```

Here is the final part of the code:

```
ubuntu@ubuntu-armhf: ~/track
File Edit Options Buffers Tools Python Help
distance = calcDistance(xpos_goal, ypos_goal, xpos_robot, ypos_robot)
print angle
print distance
moveRobot(distance, angle)
time_start = time.time()
while 1:
    x = ser.read(30)
#    print x
    range = findRange(x)
    if range > 0 and range < 20:
        print range
        time_stop = time.time()
            # stop the robot
        os.system("python dcmotor.py 5")
        time_ran = time_stop - time_start
        print time_ran
        while range < 100:
            x = ser.read(30)
            range = findRange(x)
        xpos_robot = xpos_robot + time_ran * math.cos(math.radians(angle))
        print xpos_robot
        ypos_robot = ypos_robot + time_ran * math.sin(math.radians(angle))
        print ypos_robot
        distance = 3
        angle = angle - 90
        if (angle < 0):
            angle += 360
        print distance
        print angle
        moveRobot(distance, angle)
        time.sleep(3)
        xpos_robot = xpos_robot + distance * math.cos(math.radians(angle))
        print xpos_robot
        ypos_robot = ypos_robot + distance * math.sin(math.radians(angle))
        print ypos_robot
        angle = calcAngle(xpos_goal, ypos_goal, xpos_robot, ypos_robot)
        distance = calcDistance(xpos_goal, ypos_goal, xpos_robot, ypos_robot)
        print distance
        print angle
        moveRobot(distance, angle)
        time_start = time.time()

-=--:----F1  obstacle.py    Bot L64    (Python)----------------------------------
```

The final step would be to have the robot move forward until the sensor on the side with the barrier reports that the barrier is no longer there. Then have the robot calculate its new location, then the optimum path to the goal.

As noted, there are a number of different algorithms for path planning, each with different degrees of complexity. You might want to explore the environment before deciding which way to turn. These more complex algorithms can be explored using the basic functionality that you have built in this chapter.

# Summary

In this chapter, you added to your robot an array of sensors to avoid obstacles, and a digital compass so that you can plan your route. You also learned some simple route planning techniques so that your robot can reach a goal location.

In the next chapter, we'll add vision to your robot, so you can know even more about your surrounding. You'll learn to how to detect not only color but also motion; these can be used to provide control of your robot as it moves.

# 4

# Vision and Image Processing

Now that your tracked platform can move around, you'll want to add a more complex sensor to provide information to it — the webcam. Using a webcam, you can allow your robot to see its environment. You'll learn how to use a powerful open source software platform called OpenCV to add powerful vision algorithms to your robotic platform.

In this chapter, you will be doing the following:

- Connecting a webcam
- Learning image processing using OpenCV
- Discovering edge detection for barrier finding
- Adding color and motion detection for targeting

## Connecting a webcam to the BeagleBone Black

In order to enable computer vision, you'll need to connect a USB web camera to the USB port. Most standard USB webcams will work. This example uses a Logitech HD 720.

Here are the steps:

1. Check if your USB webcam is connected. You'll do this using a program called `guvcview`. Install this by typing `sudo apt-get install guvcview`.

2. Connect your USB camera and power up the BeagleBone Black. After the system is booted, go to the `/dev` directory and type `ls`. You should see the following screenshot:

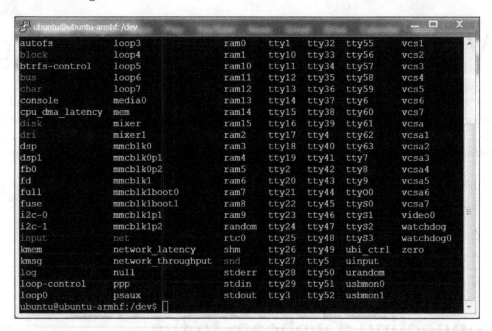

3. The `video0` device is the USB webcam. If you see its entry in the directory, then it means the system can access your camera.

Now you can use `guvcview` to see images from the camera. Since these are graphic images, you'll need to use either a monitor connected directly to the BeagleBone Black or the remote graphics connection VNC server. If you want to use the remote connection, make sure you start the server on the BeagleBone Black by typing `vncserver` via SSH. Then start VNC viewer as described in *Chapter 1, Preparing the BeagleBone Black*. Once you have a VNC viewer window, then open a terminal and type `sudo guvcview`. You should see an output similar to the following screenshot:

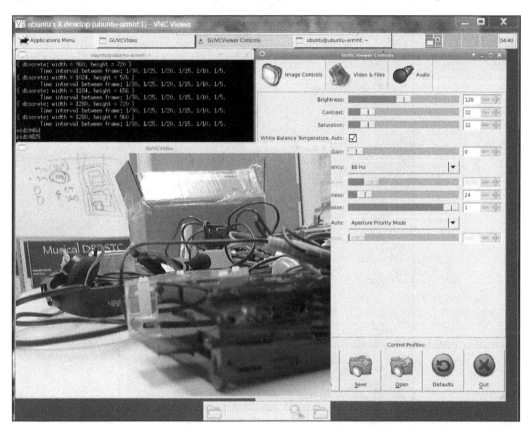

The video window displays the webcam images and the **GUVCViewer Controls** window controls the output from the camera. The default settings may work fine for your USB webcam. However, if you get a black display for the camera images, you will need to adjust the settings. Select the **GUVCViewer Controls** window and then the **Video & Files** tab. You will see a set of selections where you can adjust the settings for your camera:

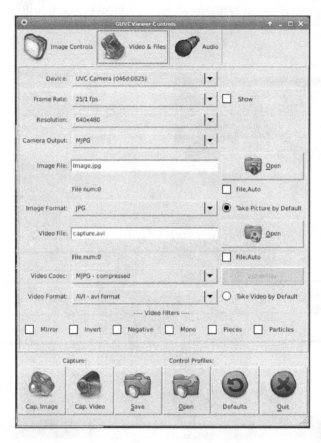

The setting that will affect your image the most is the **Resolution** setting. If you cannot see an image, then adjust the resolution down; often this will resolve the issue. The **Resolution** selection will tell you what resolutions are supported for your camera. If you want to display the frame rate, you can do it by checking the **Show** box at the right of the **Frame Rate** setting. Beware that the VNC viewer will also affect the refresh rate, so if you are doing this through the VNC viewer, your frame rate will be much slower than if you're using the BeagleBone Black and a monitor directly.

With your camera up and running and a desired resolution set, you can now start using OpenCV to process the image.

# Using OpenCV

With your camera connected, you can access amazing vision capabilities that have been provided by the open source community. One of the most powerful capabilities is OpenCV.

You already installed OpenCV in *Chapter 1, Preparing the BeagleBone Black*. If you'd like a good overview on OpenCV and more documentation, see `http://docs.opencv.org/`.

Now you can try OpenCV. It is easiest to use Python when programming simple tasks, so let's start with the Python examples. If you prefer the C examples, they are also available. In order to use the Python examples, you'll need the python-numpy library. Type `sudo apt-get install python-numpy`. You will need this to manipulate the matrices that OpenCV uses to hold the images.

Start with one of the Python examples. You can access the Python examples by typing `cd /home/ubuntu/examples/python`. There are a number of useful examples; you'll start with the most basic. It is called `camera.py`. To run this example, you'll either need to have a display connected to the BeagleBone Black, or you can do this over the VNC server connection. Bring up a terminal window and type `python camera.py`. You should see an output similar to this screenshot:

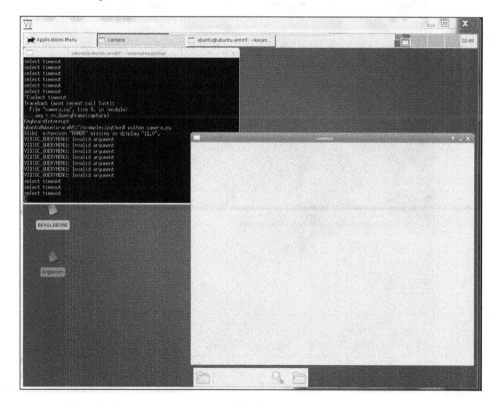

When I first did this, the camera window eventually turned black and did not show the output from the camera. To actually see the image, I needed to change the resolution of the image captured by the USB webcam to one supported by the camera and OpenCV. To do this, you need to edit the `camera.py` file by adding two lines like this:

```
File Edit Options Buffers Tools Python Help
import cv2.cv as cv
import time

cv.NamedWindow("camera", 1)

capture = cv.CaptureFromCAM(0)
cv.SetCaptureProperty(capture, 3, 360)
cv.SetCaptureProperty(capture, 4, 240)

while True:
    img = cv.QueryFrame(capture)
    cv.ShowImage("camera", img)
    if cv.WaitKey(10) == 27:
        break

-=--:----F1  camera.py      All L1      (Python)-------------------------------
For information about GNU Emacs and the GNU system, type C-h C-a.
```

These two lines change the resolution of the captured image to 360 x 240 pixels. Now run `camera.py` and you should be able to see the following screenshot:

You should now have vision capability! You will use it to do a number of impressive tasks. You may want to vary the resolution to find the optimum for your application. Larger resolution images give you a more detailed view of the world, but they also take up significantly more memory and processing power. An image that is twice the size (width/height) will involve four times more memory and processing power.

# Finding colored objects in your vision system

OpenCV can be used to track objects. As an example, let's build a system that tracks and follows a colored ball. OpenCV makes this activity amazingly simple; here are the steps:

1. Create a directory to hold your image-based work. Once you have created the directory, go there and begin with your `camera.py` file.

2. Now edit the file until it looks similar to the following screenshot:

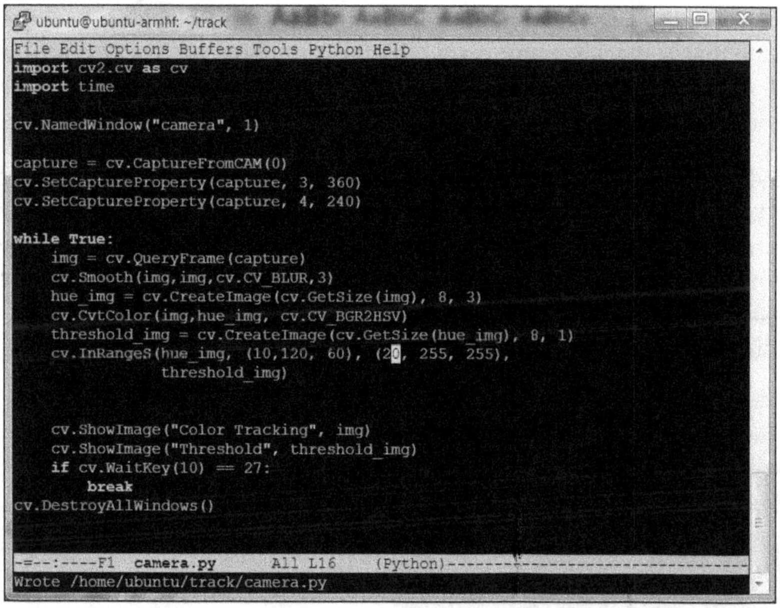

```
ubuntu@ubuntu-armhf: ~/track
File Edit Options Buffers Tools Python Help
import cv2.cv as cv
import time

cv.NamedWindow("camera", 1)

capture = cv.CaptureFromCAM(0)
cv.SetCaptureProperty(capture, 3, 360)
cv.SetCaptureProperty(capture, 4, 240)

while True:
    img = cv.QueryFrame(capture)
    cv.Smooth(img,img,cv.CV_BLUR,3)
    hue_img = cv.CreateImage(cv.GetSize(img), 8, 3)
    cv.CvtColor(img,hue_img, cv.CV_BGR2HSV)
    threshold_img = cv.CreateImage(cv.GetSize(hue_img), 8, 1)
    cv.InRangeS(hue_img, (10,120, 60), (20, 255, 255),
                threshold_img)


    cv.ShowImage("Color Tracking", img)
    cv.ShowImage("Threshold", threshold_img)
    if cv.WaitKey(10) == 27:
        break
cv.DestroyAllWindows()

-=--:----F1  camera.py      All L16    (Python)-------------------------------
Wrote /home/ubuntu/track/camera.py
```

Let's look specifically at the changes you need to make to `camera.py`. The first three lines you add are as follows:

```
cv.Smooth(img,img,cv.CV_BLUR,3)
hue_img = cv.CreateImage(cv.GetSize(img), 8, 3)
cv.CvtColor(img,hue_img, cv.CV_BGR2HSV)
```

We are going to use the OpenCV library to first smooth the image, taking out any large deviations. The next two lines create a new image that stores the image in values of **Hue (color), Saturation, and Value (HSV)** instead of the **Red, Green, and Blue (RGB)** pixel values of the original image. Converting to HSV focuses your processing more on the color as opposed to the amount of light hitting it.

3.  Then add the following lines of code:

```
#Remove all the pixels that don't match
threshold_img = cv.CreateImage(cv.GetSize(hue_img), 8, 1)
  cv.InRangeS(hue_img, (10,120, 60), (20, 255, 255),
  threshold_img)
```

You are going to create one more image, this time a black-and-white binary image that is black for any pixel which is not between two certain color values. The `(10, 160, 60), (20, 255, 255)` parameter determines the range of colors. In this case, I have an orange ball and I want to detect the color orange.

Now run the program. You can either have a display, keyboard, and mouse connected to the board, or you can run it remotely using VNC. Run the program by typing `sudo python camera.py`. You should see a single black image, but when you move this window, you will expose the original image window as well. Now take your target (I used my orange ball) and move it to the front of the frame. You should see an output similar to the following screenshot:

Notice the white pixels in your threshold image showing where the ball is located. You can add more OpenCV code that gives the actual location of the ball. You can actually draw a rectangle around the ball in your original image file as an indicator of the location of the ball. Edit the `camera.py` file to look like the following screenshot:

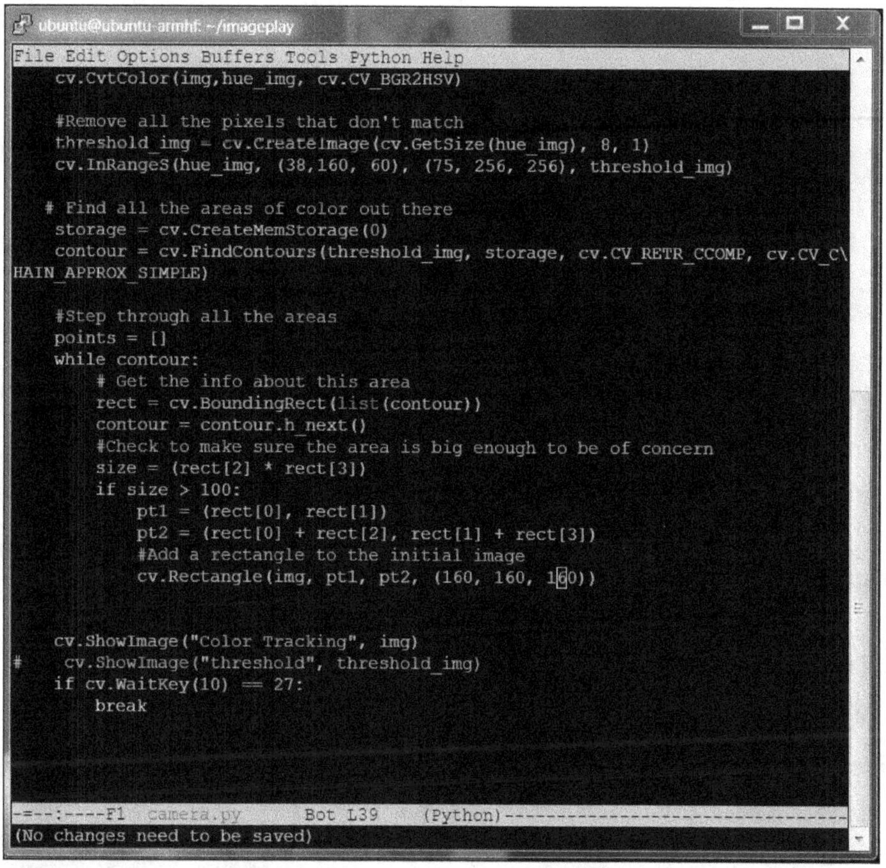

```
ubuntu@ubuntu-armhf: ~/imageplay                              _  □  X
File Edit Options Buffers Tools Python Help
    cv.CvtColor(img,hue_img, cv.CV_BGR2HSV)

    #Remove all the pixels that don't match
    threshold_img = cv.CreateImage(cv.GetSize(hue_img), 8, 1)
    cv.InRangeS(hue_img, (38,160, 60), (75, 256, 256), threshold_img)

    # Find all the areas of color out there
    storage = cv.CreateMemStorage(0)
    contour = cv.FindContours(threshold_img, storage, cv.CV_RETR_CCOMP, cv.CV_C\
HAIN_APPROX_SIMPLE)

    #Step through all the areas
    points = []
    while contour:
        # Get the info about this area
        rect = cv.BoundingRect(list(contour))
        contour = contour.h_next()
        #Check to make sure the area is big enough to be of concern
        size = (rect[2] * rect[3])
        if size > 100:
            pt1 = (rect[0], rect[1])
            pt2 = (rect[0] + rect[2], rect[1] + rect[3])
            #Add a rectangle to the initial image
            cv.Rectangle(img, pt1, pt2, (160, 160, 160))


    cv.ShowImage("Color Tracking", img)
#    cv.ShowImage("threshold", threshold_img)
    if cv.WaitKey(10) == 27:
        break



-=--:----F1  camera.py        Bot L39      (Python)-------------------
(No changes need to be saved)
```

First, add these lines:

```
storage = cv.CreateMemStorage(0)
contour = cv.FindContours(threshold_img, storage, cv.CV_
RETR_CCOMP, cv.CV_CHAIN_APPROX_SIMPLE)
```

These lines find all the areas on your image that are within the threshold. There might be more than one; so you'll want to capture them all. Now add a `while` loop that will let you step through all the possible contours:

```
points = []
while contour:
```

It is important to note that if there is another larger orange blob in the background, you will find that location. Just to keep it simple, you'll assume your orange ball to be unique. The next few lines will then get the information for each of your contours. Now you have to identify the corners. Then you can check to see if the area is big enough to be of concern. If it is, you will add a rectangle to your original image identifying where you think it is:

```
rect = cv.BoundingRect(list(contour))
contour = contour.h_next()
size = (rect[2] * rect[3])
if size > 100:
  pt1 = (rect[0], rect[1])
  pt2 = (rect[0] + rect[2], rect[1] + rect[3])
  #Add a rectangle to the initial image
  cv.Rectangle(img, pt1, pt2, (38, 160, 60))
```

Now that the code is ready, you can run it. You should see an output similar to the following screenshot:

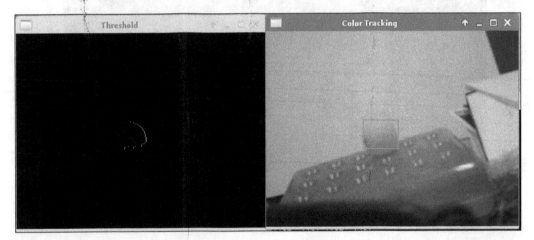

You can now track your object. Now that you have the code, you can modify the color or add more colors. You also have the location of your object, so now you can attempt to follow the object or manipulate it in some way.

# Following colored objects with your vision system

Now that your robot can sense colored objects, let's take this a step forward and use this capability to actually guide your robot. If you look at the code from the last section, you'll notice two variables, `pt1` and `pt2`. These variables hold the *x* and *y* coordinates of the color that your robot found. We can use these with our `dcmotor.py` program to move the robot so that when the color reaches the edge of the viewing area, the robot will move to put the colored object back into the middle of the viewing area. Here is the code:

```
ubuntu@ubuntu-armhf: ~/track
File Edit Options Buffers Tools Python Help
import cv2.cv as cv
import time
import os
cv.NamedWindow("camera", 1)
capture = cv.CaptureFromCAM(0)
cv.SetCaptureProperty(capture, 3, 360)
cv.SetCaptureProperty(capture, 4, 240)
time_start = time.time()
time.sleep(1)
while True:
    img = cv.QueryFrame(capture)
    cv.Smooth(img,img,cv.CV_BLUR,3)
    hue_img = cv.CreateImage(cv.GetSize(img), 8, 3)
    cv.CvtColor(img,hue_img, cv.CV_BGR2HSV)
    threshold_img = cv.CreateImage(cv.GetSize(hue_img), 8, 1)
    cv.InRangeS(hue_img, (10,120, 60), (20, 255, 255),
                threshold_img)
    storage = cv.CreateMemStorage(0)
    contour = cv.FindContours(threshold_img, storage, cv.CV_RETR_CCOMP, cv.CV_C\
HAIN_APPROX_SIMPLE)
    points = []
    while contour:
        rect = cv.BoundingRect(list(contour))
        contour = contour.h_next()
        size = (rect[2] * rect[3])
        if size > 100:
            pt1 = (rect[0], rect[1])
            pt2 = (rect[0] + rect[2], rect[1] + rect[3])
            cv.Rectangle(img, pt1, pt2, (38, 160, 60))
            time_now = time.time()
            if time_now - time_start > 1:
                if rect[0] < 20:
                    print "moving right"
                    os.system("python dcmotor.py 3 .5&")
                    time.sleep(.5)
                    time_start = time.time()
                if (rect[0] + rect[2]) > 310:
                    print "moving left"
                    os.system("python dcmotor.py 4 .5&")
                    time.sleep(.5)
                    time_start = time.time()

    cv.ShowImage("Color Tracking", img)
    if cv.WaitKey(10) == 27:
        break
-=--:**--F1   camera.py      Top L37    (Python)----------------------
```

When your robot finds a color, it also finds the *x* boundaries of that color. These are held in the `rect[0]` and `rect[2]` variables. Each time through the loop, your program checks to see if the left side is smaller than 20 or the right side is larger than 310. In either case, your program will call the `dcmotor.py` program you wrote earlier and move the robot in a turn either to the right or left. As you move the target, the robot should turn with the object. The `time_start` and `time_now` variables allow you to slow the response of your robot. Otherwise, it will overturn. You might want to comment out the `cvShowImage` statement if your robot is struggling to keep up with the movement, as this statement does take some time.

You can also use the size of the color ball to decide how far the ball is, and then move the robot forward or backwards based on this size. Here is the `while` loop for that code, and it is the only part of the code you'll need to change:

```
        cv.InRangeS(hue_img, (10,120, 60), (20, 255, 255),
                       threshold_img)
        storage = cv.CreateMemStorage(0)
        contour = cv.FindContours(threshold_img, storage, cv.CV_RETR_CCOMP, cv.CV_C\
HAIN_APPROX_SIMPLE)
        points = []
        while contour:
            rect = cv.BoundingRect(list(contour))
            contour = contour.h_next()
            size = (rect[2] * rect[3])
            if size > 100:
                pt1 = (rect[0], rect[1])
                pt2 = (rect[0] + rect[2], rect[1] + rect[3])
                #Add a rectangle to the initial image
                cv.Rectangle(img, pt1, pt2, (38, 160, 60))
                print rect[0], rect[0] + rect[2], rect[2]
                time_now = time.time()
                if time_now - time_start > 1:
                    if rect[0] < 10:
                        print "moving right"
                        os.system("python dcmotor.py 3 .5&")
                        time.sleep(.5)
                        time_start = time.time()
                    if (rect[0] + rect[2]) > 310:
                        print "moving left"
                        os.system("python dcmotor.py 4 .5&")
                        time.sleep(.5)
                        time_start = time.time()
                    if rect[2] > 60:
                        print "backing up"
                        os.system("python dcmotor.py 1 .5&")
                        time.sleep(.5)
                        time_start = time.time()
                    if rect[2] < 40:
                        print "moving forward"
                        os.system("python dcmotor.py 2 .5&")
                        time.sleep(.5)
                        time_start = time.time()

        cv.ShowImage("Color Tracking", img)
        if cv.WaitKey(10) == 27:
            break
cv.DestroyAllWindows()
```

The changes are simple. You will check the value of rect[2] which is the size of the color rectangle. If it is large enough, you move backward. If it is small enough, you will move forward.

# Finding movement in your vision system

Another interesting behavior of your tracked robot is the ability to find motion. Here is the first part of the code to use the OpenCV library and your webcam to follow motion:

```python
#!/usr/bin/env python

import cv
capture = cv.CaptureFromCAM(0)
cv.NamedWindow("Target", 1)
# Capture first frame to get size
frame = cv.QueryFrame(capture)
frame_size = cv.GetSize(frame)
color_image = cv.CreateImage(cv.GetSize(frame), 8, 3)
grey_image = cv.CreateImage(cv.GetSize(frame), cv.IPL_DEPTH_8U, 1)
moving_average = cv.CreateImage(cv.GetSize(frame), cv.IPL_DEPTH_32F, 3)
first = True
while True:
    color_image = cv.QueryFrame(capture)
    cv.Smooth(color_image, color_image, cv.CV_GAUSSIAN, 3, 0)
    if first:
        difference = cv.CloneImage(color_image)
        temp = cv.CloneImage(color_image)
        cv.ConvertScale(color_image, moving_average, 1.0, 0.0)
        first = False
    else:
        cv.RunningAvg(color_image, moving_average, 0.020, None)
    cv.ConvertScale(moving_average, temp, 1.0, 0.0)
    cv.AbsDiff(color_image, temp, difference)
    cv.CvtColor(difference, grey_image, cv.CV_RGB2GRAY)
    cv.Threshold(grey_image, grey_image, 70, 255, cv.CV_THRESH_BINARY)
    cv.Dilate(grey_image, grey_image, None, 18)
    cv.Erode(grey_image, grey_image, None, 10)
    storage = cv.CreateMemStorage(0)
    contour = cv.FindContours(grey_image, storage, cv.CV_RETR_CCOMP, cv.CV_CHAIN_APPROX_SIMPLE)
    points = []
    while contour:
        bound_rect = cv.BoundingRect(list(contour))
        contour = contour.h_next()
        pt1 = (bound_rect[0], bound_rect[1])
        pt2 = (bound_rect[0] + bound_rect[2], bound_rect[1] + bound_rect[3])
        points.append(pt1)
        points.append(pt2)
        cv.Rectangle(color_image, pt1, pt2, cv.CV_RGB(255,0,0), 1)
    if len(points):
        center_point = reduce(lambda a, b: ((a[0] + b[0]) / 2, (a[1] + b[1]) / 2), points)
        cv.Circle(color_image, center_point, 40, cv.CV_RGB(255, 255, 255), 1)
        cv.Circle(color_image, center_point, 30, cv.CV_RGB(255, 100, 0), 1)
        cv.Circle(color_image, center_point, 20, cv.CV_RGB(255, 255, 255), 1)
```

The following is the second part of the code to use the OpenCV library and your webcam to follow motion:

```
ubuntu@ubuntu-armhf: ~/track
File Edit Options Buffers Tools Python Help
frame_size = cv.GetSize(frame)
color_image = cv.CreateImage(cv.GetSize(frame), 8, 3)
grey_image = cv.CreateImage(cv.GetSize(frame), cv.IPL_DEPTH_8U, 1)
moving_average = cv.CreateImage(cv.GetSize(frame), cv.IPL_DEPTH_32F, 3)
first = True
while True:
    color_image = cv.QueryFrame(capture)
    cv.Smooth(color_image, color_image, cv.CV_GAUSSIAN, 3, 0)
    if first:
        difference = cv.CloneImage(color_image)
        temp = cv.CloneImage(color_image)
        cv.ConvertScale(color_image, moving_average, 1.0, 0.0)
        first = False
    else:
        cv.RunningAvg(color_image, moving_average, 0.020, None)
    cv.ConvertScale(moving_average, temp, 1.0, 0.0)
    cv.AbsDiff(color_image, temp, difference)
    cv.CvtColor(difference, grey_image, cv.CV_RGB2GRAY)
    cv.Threshold(grey_image, grey_image, 70, 255, cv.CV_THRESH_BINARY)
    cv.Dilate(grey_image, grey_image, None, 18)
    cv.Erode(grey_image, grey_image, None, 10)
    storage = cv.CreateMemStorage(0)
    contour = cv.FindContours(grey_image, storage, cv.CV_RETR_CCOMP, cv.CV_CHAIN_APPROX_SIMPLE)
    points = []
    while contour:
        bound_rect = cv.BoundingRect(list(contour))
        contour = contour.h_next()
        pt1 = (bound_rect[0], bound_rect[1])
        pt2 = (bound_rect[0] + bound_rect[2], bound_rect[1] + bound_rect[3])
        points.append(pt1)
        points.append(pt2)
        cv.Rectangle(color_image, pt1, pt2, cv.CV_RGB(255,0,0), 1)
    if len(points):
        center_point = reduce(lambda a, b: ((a[0] + b[0]) / 2, (a[1] + b[1]) / 2), points)
        cv.Circle(color_image, center_point, 40, cv.CV_RGB(255, 255, 255), 1)
        cv.Circle(color_image, center_point, 30, cv.CV_RGB(255, 100, 0), 1)
        cv.Circle(color_image, center_point, 20, cv.CV_RGB(255, 255, 255), 1)
        cv.Circle(color_image, center_point, 10, cv.CV_RGB(255, 100, 0), 1)
    cv.ShowImage("Target", color_image)
    # Listen for ESC key
    c = cv.WaitKey(7) % 0x100
    if c == 27:
        break
-=--:----F1  motion.py      Bot L30     (Python)---------------------------------
```

It is useful to look at the code in detail. This first section of the code is very similar to the setup code you used in the colored object section:

- `#!/usr/bin/env python`: This line allows the program to be executed as a regular program.

- `import cv`: This line imports the OpenCV library.

- `capture = cv.CaptureFromCAM(0)`: This opens the connection to `webcam(0)`.

- `cv.NamedWindow("Target", 1)`: This creates a window on the display with the name as `Target`.

- `frame = cv.QueryFrame(capture)`: This grabs an image from the webcam and sticks it in the variable frame.

- `frame_size = cv.GetSize(frame)`: This returns the frame size of the image as a tuple (set of two numbers) of width and height.

- `color_image = cv.CreateImage(cv.GetSize(frame), 8, 3)`: This creates a color image from the frame and puts it into the `color_image` variable. You can use it later to display the image.

- `grey_image = cv.CreateImage(cv.GetSize(frame), cv.IPL_DEPTH_8U, 1)`: This creates a grey-scale image of the frame and puts it into the `grey_image` variable. You'll use this image to detect changes in the image.

- `moving_average = cv.CreateImage(cv.GetSize(frame), cv.IPL_DEPTH_32F, 3)`: This creates an image of the frame using just the real values and puts it into the `moving_average` variable. You'll use this image to detect changes in the image.

- `first = True`: This sets the variable `first` to `True`, as in this is the first image.

The second section enters a loop and looks for changes in the images:

- `while True`: This is an infinite loop.

- `color_image = cv.QueryFrame(capture)`: This grabs an image from the webcam and sticks it in the variable frame.

- `cv.Smooth(color_image, color_image, cv.CV_GAUSSIAN, 3, 0)`: This smoothens the image using a Gaussian filter, taking out large color deviations in the image.

- `if first`: This checks whether the image is the first image.

- `difference = cv.CloneImage(color_image)`: This creates another variable called `difference` and stores a copy of `color_image` into that variable.

- `temp = cv.CloneImage(color_image)`: This creates another variable called `temp` and stores a copy of `color_image` into that variable.

- `cv.ConvertScale(color_image, moving_average, 1.0, 0.0)`: This makes sure that the sizes of `color_image` and `moving_average` are of the same scale.

- `first = False`: This is set to `False` since this is no longer the first time through the loop.

- `else`: This states that if this is not the first image, you can actually do a running average on the video stream.

- `cv.RunningAvg(color_image, moving_average, 0.020, None)`:
  The `RunningAvg` function adds the `color_image` frame into a moving average. This creates a composite frame that looks at a set of frames as an average of the individual frames.

- `cv.ConvertScale(moving_average, temp, 1.0, 0.0)`: This makes sure that the sizes of `color_image` and `moving_average` are of the same scale.

- `cv.AbsDiff(color_image, temp, difference)`: This calculates the absolute difference between `color_image` and `temp` and stores this difference in the `difference` variable.

- `cv.CvtColor(difference, grey_image, cv.CV_RGB2GRAY)`:
  This converts the color difference image into a black and white image and stores it in `grey_image`.

- `cv.Threshold(grey_image, grey_image, 70, 255, cv.CV_THRESH_BINARY)`: This highlights the areas of the display that are significantly different by turning on only those pixels that are above a certain threshold of white.

- `cv.Dilate(grey_image, grey_image, None, 18)`: This dilates the grey image, emphasizing the areas where there is a white area.

- `cv.Erode(grey_image, grey_image, None, 10)`: This erodes the black-and-white image, again emphasizing the areas of change. For more information on dilation and erosion, see `http://docs.opencv.org/doc/tutorials/imgproc/erosion_dilatation/erosion_dilatation.html`.

- `storage = cv.CreateMemStorage(0)`: This creates a storage area so that you can identify the areas of a color.

- `contour = cv.FindContours(grey_image, storage, cv.CV_RETR_CCOMP, cv.CV_CHAIN_APPROX_SIMPLE)`; This is a contour that finds those areas of the image that have groups of pixels that indicate change.

- `points = []`: This creates an array where you can put the location of the areas of pixel that indicate change.

- `while contour`: This walks through each contour, locating the areas of the movement.

- `bound_rect = cv.BoundingRect(list(contour))`: This holds the values of the bounding rectangle around the contour of movement. It has four points: `bound_rect[0]` holds the $x$ value of the rectangle that contains the area of movement, `bound_rect[1]` holds the $y$ value of the rectangle that contains the area of movement, `bound_rect[2]` holds the width of a rectangle that contains the area of movement, and `bound_rect[3]` holds the height of the rectangle that contains the area of movement.

- `contour = contour.h_next()`: This prepares the program to process the next contour that indicates the movement.

- `pt1 = (bound_rect[0], bound_rect[1])`: This creates a `pt1` variable that holds the *x* and *y* values of the upper-left corner of the contour.

- `pt2 = (bound_rect[0] + bound_rect[2], bound_rect[1] + bound_rect[3])`: This creates a `pt2` variable that holds the *x* and *y* values of the lower-right corner of the contour.

- `points.append(pt1)`: This puts the points of this rectangle's *x* and *y* upper-left values on the array of points.

- `points.append(pt2)`: This puts the points of this rectangle's *x* and *y* lower-right values on the array of points.

- `cv.Rectangle(color_image, pt1, pt2, cv.CV_RGB(255,0,0), 1)`: This draws a rectangle on the original image of this particular rectangle of movement.

- `if len(points)`: If there are any rectangles, then perform this set of instructions.

- `center_point = reduce(lambda a, b: ((a[0] + b[0]) / 2, (a[1] + b[1]) / 2), points)`: This finds the center point for all of the rectangles in this list. It also finds all of the movement rectangles and calculates the center point for all of the movement rectangles.

- `cv.Circle(color_image, center_point, 40, cv.CV_RGB(255, 255, 255), 1)`: This draws a circle on the original image with a radius of 40, to indicate the center of the movement.

- `cv.Circle(color_image, center_point, 30, cv.CV_RGB(255, 100, 0), 1)`: This draws a circle on the original image with a radius of 30, to indicate the center of the movement.

- `cv.Circle(color_image, center_point, 20, cv.CV_RGB(255, 255, 255), 1)`: This draws a circle on the original image with a radius of 20, to indicate the center of the movement.

- `cv.Circle(color_image, center_point, 10, cv.CV_RGB(255, 100, 0), 1)`: This draws a circle on the original image with a radius of 10, to indicate the center of the movement.

- `cv.ShowImage("Target", color_image)`: This draws the original image, with the movement rectangles and the center of the movement circles on the screen.

- `# Listen for ESC key`: This is a comment to listen for the ESC key.

- `c = cv.WaitKey(7) % 0x100`: This listens for the *Esc* key, and stops the program if it is selected. This is also required if you want to display your image.
- `if c == 27`: This checks whether the ESC key (key 27) is pressed or not.
- `break`: This stops the program.

If you run the code and supply some movement, you should see something like this:

Now that you can sense movement, you can also program your robot to follow it. As with the previous program, each time through the loop, your program checks to see if the movement is with 20 pixels on the right or left side. In either case, your program will call the `dcmotor.py` program you wrote earlier and move the robot in a turn either to the right or left. Again, as before, you might want to comment out the `cvShowImage` line and the `print` statements if your robot is struggling to keep up with the movement, as these statements do take some time.

# Following movement with your robot

To follow the movement, you will do something very similar to the previous section on following color. Your program will hold the center of the movement in the `center_point` variable, which will hold and the *x* and *y* value. You can then use it to move your robot if it is on either edge of the vision field. The first additions you'll need to add to your program are the `import time` and `import os` lines at the top of the file, to include these libraries. Here are the changes:

```
ubuntu@ubuntu-armhf: ~/track
File Edit Options Buffers Tools Python Help
#!/usr/bin/env python
import time
import cv
import os
capture = cv.CaptureFromCAM(0)
cv.NamedWindow("Target", 1)
# Capture first frame to get size
frame = cv.QueryFrame(capture)
frame_size = cv.GetSize(frame)
color_image = cv.CreateImage(cv.GetSize(frame), 8, 3)
grey_image = cv.CreateImage(cv.GetSize(frame), cv.IPL_DEPTH_8U, 1)
moving_average = cv.CreateImage(cv.GetSize(frame), cv.IPL_DEPTH_32F, 3)
first = True
time_start = time.time()
while True:
    color_image = cv.QueryFrame(capture)
    cv.Smooth(color_image, color_image, cv.CV_GAUSSIAN, 3, 0)
    if first:
        difference = cv.CloneImage(color_image)
        temp = cv.CloneImage(color_image)
        cv.ConvertScale(color_image, moving_average, 1.0, 0.0)
        first = False
    else:
        cv.RunningAvg(color_image, moving_average, 0.020, None)
    cv.ConvertScale(moving_average, temp, 1.0, 0.0)
    cv.AbsDiff(color_image, temp, difference)
    cv.CvtColor(difference, grey_image, cv.CV_RGB2GRAY)
    cv.Threshold(grey_image, grey_image, 70, 255, cv.CV_THRESH_BINARY)
    cv.Dilate(grey_image, grey_image, None, 18)
    cv.Erode(grey_image, grey_image, None, 10)
    storage = cv.CreateMemStorage(0)
    contour = cv.FindContours(grey_image, storage, cv.CV_RETR_CCOMP, cv.CV_CHA\
IN_APPROX_SIMPLE)
    points = []
```

Here are the main additions at the bottom of the program on motion detection:

```
ubuntu@ubuntu-armhf: ~/track
File Edit Options Buffers Tools Python Help
    cv.ConvertScale(moving_average, temp, 1.0, 0.0)
    cv.AbsDiff(color_image, temp, difference)
    cv.CvtColor(difference, grey_image, cv.CV_RGB2GRAY)
    cv.Threshold(grey_image, grey_image, 70, 255, cv.CV_THRESH_BINARY)
    cv.Dilate(grey_image, grey_image, None, 18)
    cv.Erode(grey_image, grey_image, None, 10)
    storage = cv.CreateMemStorage(0)
    contour = cv.FindContours(grey_image, storage, cv.CV_RETR_CCOMP, cv.CV_CHA\
IN_APPROX_SIMPLE)
    points = []
    while contour:
        bound_rect = cv.BoundingRect(list(contour))
        contour = contour.h_next()
        pt1 = (bound_rect[0], bound_rect[1])
        pt2 = (bound_rect[0] + bound_rect[2], bound_rect[1] + bound_rect[3])
        points.append(pt1)
        points.append(pt2)
        cv.Rectangle(color_image, pt1, pt2, cv.CV_RGB(255,0,0), 1)
    if len(points):
        center_point = reduce(lambda a, b: ((a[0] + b[0]) / 2, (a[1] + b[1]) /\
2), points)
        cv.Circle(color_image, center_point, 40, cv.CV_RGB(255, 255, 255), 1)
        cv.Circle(color_image, center_point, 30, cv.CV_RGB(255, 100, 0), 1)
        cv.Circle(color_image, center_point, 20, cv.CV_RGB(255, 255, 255), 1)
        cv.Circle(color_image, center_point, 10, cv.CV_RGB(255, 100, 0), 1)
        time_now = time.time()
        if time_now - time_start > 2:
            if center_point[0] < 50:
                print "moving right"
                os.system("python dcmotor.py 3 .5&")
                time.sleep(.5)
                time_start = time.time()
            if center_point[0] > 300:
                print "moving left"
                os.system("python dcmotor.py 4 .5&")
                time.sleep(.5)
                time_start = time.time()

    cv.ShowImage("Target", color_image)
    # Listen for ESC key
    c = cv.WaitKey(7) % 0x100
    if c == 27:
        break

-=--:----F1  motionMove.py   Bot L45    (Python)-----------------------------
```

These lines should look almost exactly like the lines you added to move your robot when tracking color. The timing statements prevent our robot from overreacting to the movement. Now your robot should be able to follow movement within its field of vision.

# Summary

In this chapter, your robot added a video camera and video processing so that it can really see its environment. Now that your robot can move and fully sense its environment, feel free to explore, literally. In the next chapter, you'll start on a new robot. You'll build a robot that can walk on four legs; a quadruped that will walk instead of rolling. You'll learn how to control multiple servos to make your robot walk, wave, and dance.

# 5
# Building a Robot that Can Walk

You've built robots that can navigate using tracks. Now let's build one that can walk. Walking robots are interesting as they can go to terrains where wheeled or tracked vehicles can't go. They also perform advanced functions where they can utilize their legs for uses other than walking.

In this chapter, you will build the basic platform of a quadruped. To do this, you will learn the following:

- The working of servos
- Using the BeagleBone Black to control a large number of servos with the help of a servo controller
- Creating complex movements out of simple servo commands

## Building robots that can walk

In this chapter, you'll build a quadruped, that is, a robot with four legs. You'll be using 12 servos so that each leg has three points that can move, or three **Degrees of Freedom (DOF)**. In *Chapter 6, A Robot that Can Sail*, you'll learn how to control servomotors directly using the GPIO pins of the BeagleBone Black. In this project, you'll control 12 servos at the same time, so it will make more sense to use an external servo controller that can supply the control signals and supply voltages for all the 12 servos.

Since servos are the main component of this project, it is perhaps useful to go through a tutorial on servos and how to control them.

# Working of servomotors

Servomotors are somewhat similar to DC motors; however, there is an important difference. While DC motors are generally designed to move in a continuous way—rotating 360 degrees at a given speed—servos are generally designed to move within a limited set of angles

In other words, in the case of a DC motor, you would generally want your motors to spin with continuous rotation speed that you control. But in the case of a servomotor, you would want your motor to move to a specific position that you control. This is done by sending a **Pulse-Width-Modulated** (**PWM**) signal to the control connector of the servo. PWM simply means that you are going to change the length of each pulse of electrical energy in order to control something. In this case, the length of this pulse will control the angle of the servo, as shown in the following diagram:

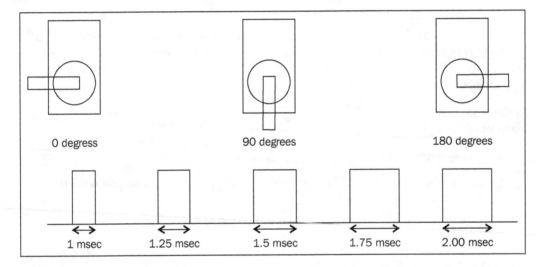

These pulses are sent out with a repetition rate of 60 Hz. You can position the servo to any angle by setting the correct control pulse.

# Building the quadruped platform

You'll first need some parts so that you can build your quadruped robot. There are several kit possibilities out there, including the one available at www. trossenrobotics.com/p/PhantomX-AX-12-Quadruped.aspx. However, such kits can be expensive, so for this example, you'll create your own kit using a set of Lynxmotion parts. These are available from several online retailers such as robotshop.com. To build this quadruped, you'll need four legs, each leg requires two Lynxmotion parts. Here are the parts with their Robotshop part numbers:

| Quantity | Description |
| --- | --- |
| 1 | Lynxmotion symmetric quadruped body kit: Mini QBK-02 |
| 2 | Lynxmotion 3" aluminum femur pair |
| 2 | Lynxmotion Robot Leg "A" pair (No servo) RL-01 |
| 4 | Lynxmotion aluminum multi-purpose servo bracket Two Pack ASB-04 |
| 2 | Ball bearing with flange: 3mm ID (pair) |
| | Product code: RB-Lyn-317 |

This last part  a bearing you'll need to connect the leg to the body.

You'll also need 12 servos of a standard size. There are several possible choices, but I personally like the **Hitec** servos. They are very inexpensive and you can get them from most hobby shops and online electronic retailers. Now, for a moment on the model of servo: Servos come in different model numbers, primarily based on the amount of torque they can generate.

**Torque** is the force that the servo can exert to move the part connected to it. In this case, your servos will need to lift and move the weight associated with your quadruped, so you'll need a servo with enough torque to do this. I suggest that you use eight Hitec model HS-485HB servos. You'll use these for the servos attached to the end of the leg and for the body. Then you'll use four Hitec model HS-645MG servos for the middle of the leg; this is the servo that will require the highest amount of torque. You can use the 12 Hitec model HS-645MG servos instead, but they are more expensive than the HS-485 servos, so using two different servos will be less expensive.

Here are the steps required to assemble the quadruped:

1. Put the two parts of the lower right leg together and insert the servo with the servo mounting screws. It should look like this:

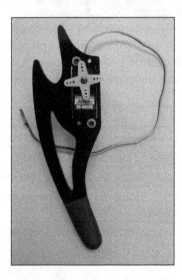

2. Now connect this assembly to the interconnect part, like this:

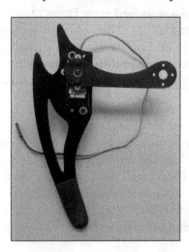

3. Complete the leg by connecting two of the servo brackets together at right angles, mounting the HS-645MG on one of the brackets, and then connecting this servo to the interconnect piece, like this:

4. Put another right leg together.

5. Now put two left legs together following the same preceding steps, but in left leg configuration. They look like this:

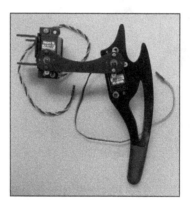

6. The next step is to build the body kit. There are some instructions given at www.lynxmotion.com/images/html/sq3u-assembly.htm, but it should be like the following image:

7. Then connect each leg to the body kit. First connect the empty servo bracket to the body using the bearing, as shown in the following image:

8. Now connect the other servo to the empty servo bracket and the body, like this:

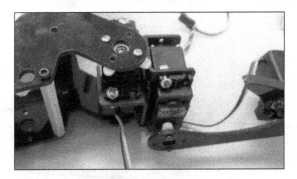

After performing all the preceding steps, your quadruped should now look like this:

Now that you have the basic hardware assembled, you can turn your attention to the electronics.

# Using a servo controller to control the servos

To make your quadruped walk, you will first need to connect the servomotor controller to the servos. The servo controller you are going to use for this project is a simple servomotor controller utilizing USB from Pololu (Pololu item number 1354, available at `pololu.com`) that can control 18 servomotors. Here is an image of the unit:

Make sure that you order the assembled version. This piece of hardware will turn USB commands from the BeagleBone Black into signals that control your servomotors. Pololu makes a number of different versions of this controller, each able to control a certain number of servos. In this case, you may want to choose the 18-servo version, so you can control all 12 servos with one controller and also add an additional servo to control the direction of a camera or sensor. You could also choose the 12-servo version. One advantage of the 18-servo controller is the ease of connecting power to the unit via screw-type connectors.

There are two connections you'll need to make to the servo controller to get started: the first is to the servomotors and the second is to a battery.

First, connect the servos to the controller. In order to be consistent, let's connect your 12 servos to the connections marked **0** through **11** on the controller using the configuration shown in the following table:

| Servo Connector | Servo |
| --- | --- |
| 0 | Right front lower leg |
| 1 | Right front middle leg |
| 2 | Right front upper leg |
| 3 | Right rear lower leg |
| 4 | Right rear middle leg |

| Servo Connector | Servo |
|---|---|
| 5 | Right rear upper leg |
| 6 | Left front lower leg |
| 7 | Left front middle leg |
| 8 | Left front upper leg |
| 9 | Left rear lower leg |
| 10 | Left rear middle leg |
| 11 | Left rear upper leg |

Here is an image of the back of the controller. This will tell us where to connect our servos:

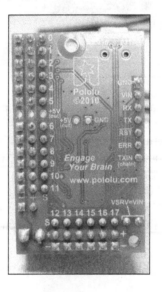

Now you need to connect the servomotor controller to your battery. For this project, you can use a 2S RC LiPo battery. The 2S means that the battery will have two cells, with an output voltage of 7.2 volts. It will supply the voltage and current needed by your servos, which can be of the order of 2 amperes. Here is an image of the battery:

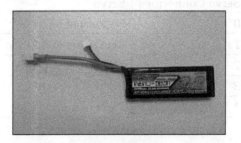

This battery will come with two connectors: one with large gauge wires for normal usage and a smaller connector used to connect to the battery recharger. You'll want to build connectors that can connect to the screw-type connectors of the servo controller. I purchased some XT60 connector pairs, soldered some wires to the mating connector of the battery, and screwed these into the servo controller.

Your system is now functional. Now you'll connect the motor controller to your personal computer to check if you can communicate with it. To do this, connect a mini USB cable between the servo controller and your personal computer.

# Communicating with the servo controller via a PC

Now that the hardware is connected, you can use some software provided by Pololu to control the servos. Let's do this using your personal computer. First download the Pololu software from `www.pololu.com/docs/0J40/3.a` and install it according to the instructions on the website. Once it is installed, run the software, and you should see something like the following screenshot:

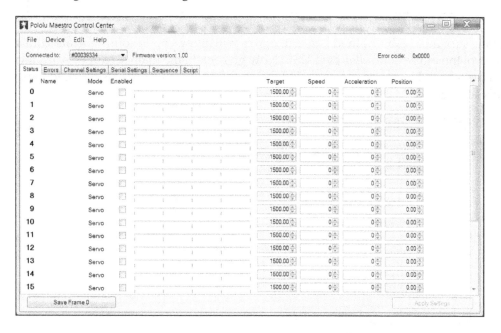

You will first need to change the configuration of the serial settings, so select the **Serial Settings** tab and you should see this:

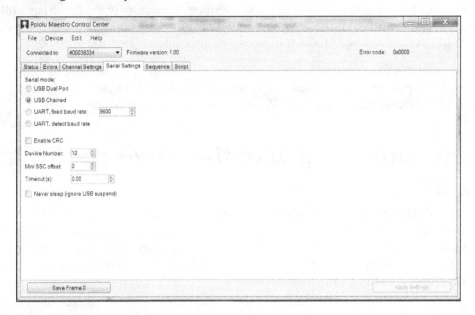

Make sure that **USB Chained** is selected; this will allow you to communicate with and control the motor controller over USB. Now go back to the main screen by selecting the **Status** tab, and now you can actually turn on the 12 servos. The screen should look like this screenshot:

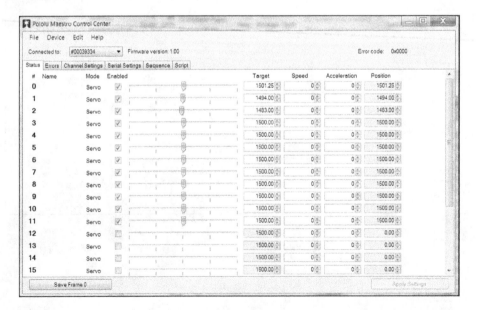

Now you can use the sliders to actually control the servos. Check that servo 0 moves the right front lower servo, servo 1 moves the right front middle servo, servo 2 moves the right front upper servo, and so on. You can also use this to center the servos. Set all the servos such that the slider is in the middle. Now unscrew the servo horn on each servo until the servos are centered at this location. At the zero degree location of all servos, your quadruped should look like this:

Your quadruped is now ready to actually do something. Now you'll need to send the servos the electronic signals they need to move your quadruped.

# Connecting the servo controller to the BeagleBone Black

You've checked the servomotor controller and the servos. You'll now connect the motor controller to the BeagleBone Black and make sure you can control the servos from it. Remove the USB cable from the PC and connect it to the BeagleBone Black. The entire system will look like this:

Let's now talk to the motor controller by downloading the Linux code from Pololu at `www.pololu.com/docs/0J40/3.b`. Perhaps the best way is to log in to your BeagleBone Black using PuTTY, then type `wget http://www.pololu.com/file/download/maestro-linux-100507.tar.gz?file_id=0J315`. Then move the file by typing `mv maestro-linux-100507.tar.gz\?file_id\=0J315 maestro-linux-100507.tar.gz`. Unpack the file by typing `tar -xzfv maestro_linux_011507.tar.gz`. This will create a directory called `maestro_linux`. Go to that directory by typing `cd maestro_linux` and then type `ls`. You should see something like this:

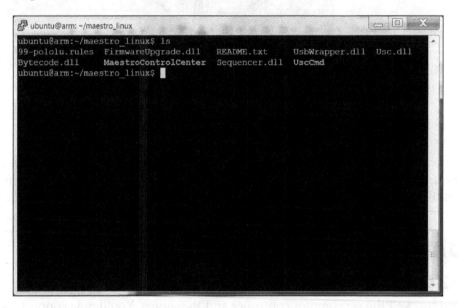

The `README.txt` document will give you explicit instructions on how to install the software. Unfortunately, you can't run `MaestroControlCenter` on your BeagleBone Black. Your version of Windows doesn't support the graphics, but you can control your servos using the `UscCmd` command-line application to ensure that they are connected and working correctly. First, type `./UscCmd --list` and you should see something like the following screenshot:

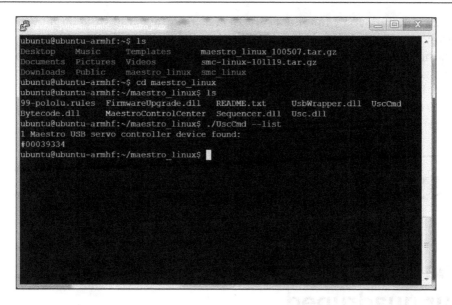

The unit sees our servo controller. By just typing ./UscCmd, you can see all the commands that you can send to your controller, as shown in the following screenshot:

Note that although you can send a servo a specific target angle, the target is not in angle values, so it makes it a bit difficult to know where you are sending your servo. Try typing ./UscCmd --servo 0, 10. The servo will move to its maximum angle position. Type ./UscCmd - servo 0, 0 and it will prevent the servo from trying to move. In the next section, you'll write some Python code that will translate your angles to the commands that the servo controller will want to receive to move it to specific angle locations.

> If you didn't run the Windows version of Maestro Controller and set the **Serial Settings** to **USB Chained**, your motor controller might not respond. Rerun the Maestro Controller code and set the **Serial Settings** to **USB Chained**.

# Creating a program on Linux to control your quadruped

You now know that you can talk to your servomotor controller, and move your servos. In this section, you'll create a Python program that will let you talk to your servos to move them to specific angles.

Let's start with a simple program that will make your legged mobile robot's servos go to 90 degrees (the middle of the 0 to 180 degrees you can set). This particular controller uses bytes of information, so the code will translate the input of the channel and angle to numbers that the controller can understand. For more details, see http://www.pololu.com/docs/0J40. Here is the code to move all the connected servos to the 90 degree point:

```
File Edit Options Buffers Tools Python Help
#!/usr/bin/python
import serial

def setAngle(ser, channel, angle):
    minAngle = 0.0
    maxAngle = 180.0
    minTarget = 256.0
    maxTarget = 13120.0
    scaledValue = int((angle / ((maxAngle - minAngle) / (maxTarget - minTarget))) + minTarget)
    commandByte = chr(0x84)
    channelByte = chr(channel)
    lowTargetByte = chr(scaledValue & 0x7F)
    highTargetByte = chr((scaledValue >> 7) & 0x7F)
    command = commandByte + channelByte + lowTargetByte + highTargetByte
    ser.write(command)
    ser.flush()

ser = serial.Serial("/dev/ttyACM0", 9600)

# Home position
for i in range(0, 15):
    setAngle(ser, i, 90)

ser.close()
```

Here is an explanation of the code:

- `#! /usr/bin/python`: This first line allows you to make this Python file executable from the command line.

- `import serial`: This line imports the serial library. You need the serial library to talk to your unit via USB.

- `def setAngle(ser, channel, angle)`: This function converts your desired setting of servo and angle into the serial command that the servomotor controller needs.

- `ser = serial.Serial("/dev/ttyACM0", 9600)`: This opens the serial port connection to your servo controller.

- `for i in range(0, 15)`: This is for all 16 servo possibilities.

- `setAngle(ser, i, 90)`: This allows you to set each servo to the middle (home) position. The default would be to set each servo to 90 degrees. If the legs of your robot aren't in their middle position, you can adjust them by adjusting the position of the servo horns on each servo.

To access the serial port, you'll need to make sure that you have the Python serial library. If you don't, then type `sudo apt-get install python-serial`. After you have installed the serial library, you can run your program by typing `sudo python quad.py`.

Once you have the basic home position set, you can now ask your robot to do some things. Let's start by making your quadruped wave an arm. Here is the Python code that waves the arm:

```python
#!/usr/bin/python
import serial
import time

def setAngle(ser, channel, angle):
    minAngle = 0.0
    maxAngle = 180.0
    minTarget = 256.0
    maxTarget = 13120.0
    scaledValue = int((angle / ((maxAngle - minAngle) / (maxTarget - minTarget))) + minTarget)
    commandByte = chr(0x84)
    channelByte = chr(channel)
    lowTargetByte = chr(scaledValue & 0x7F)
    highTargetByte = chr((scaledValue >> 7) & 0x7F)
    command = commandByte + channelByte + lowTargetByte + highTargetByte
    ser.write(command)
    ser.flush()

ser = serial.Serial("/dev/ttyACM0", 9600)

# Home position
for i in range(0, 15):
    setAngle(ser, i, 90)

setAngle(ser, 1, 110)
time.sleep(1)
setAngle(ser, 0, 130)
time.sleep(1)
setAngle(ser, 0, 100)
time.sleep(1)
setAngle(ser, 0, 130)
time.sleep(1)
setAngle(ser, 0, 100)
time.sleep(1)
setAngle(ser, 0, 90)
time.sleep(.2)
setAngle(ser, 1, 90)
ser.close()
```

In this case, you are using the `setAngle` command to set your servos to manipulate your robot's front-right arm. The middle servo raises the arm, and the lower servo then goes back and forth between angle `100` and `130`.

One of the most basic actions you'll want your robot to do is to walk forward. Here is an example of how to manipulate the legs to make this happen:

```
ser = serial.Serial("/dev/ttyACM0", 9600)

# Home position
for i in range(0, 15):
    setAngle(ser, i, 90)
time.sleep(1)

setAngle(ser, 4, 110)
time.sleep(1)
setAngle(ser, 5, 100)
time.sleep(1)
setAngle(ser, 4, 90)
time.sleep(1)

setAngle(ser, 7, 70)
time.sleep(1)
setAngle(ser, 8, 80)
time.sleep(1)
setAngle(ser, 7, 90)
time.sleep(1)

setAngle(ser, 1, 110)
time.sleep(1)
setAngle(ser, 2, 100)
time.sleep(1)
setAngle(ser, 1, 90)
time.sleep(1)

setAngle(ser, 10, 70)
time.sleep(1)
setAngle(ser, 11, 80)
time.sleep(1)
setAngle(ser, 10, 90)
time.sleep(1)

for i in range(0, 15):
    setAngle(ser, i, 90)

ser.close()
```

```
-UU-:**--F1  robot.py      Bot L38    (Python)--------------------
Auto-saving...done
```

This program lifts and moves each leg forward one at a time, and then moves all the legs to home position, which moves the robot forward. Not the most elegant motion, but it does work. There are more sophisticated algorithms to make your quadruped walk as shown at http://letsmakerobots.com/node/35354 and https://www.youtube.com/watch?v=jWP3RnYa_tw. Once you have the program working, you'll want to package all of your hardware onto the mobile robot.

You can make your robot do many amazing things: walk forward, walk backward, dance, turn around—any kinds of movements are possible. The best way to learn is to try new and different positions with the servos.

# Issuing voice commands to your quadruped

You should now have a mobile platform that you can program to move in any number of ways. Unfortunately, you still have your LAN cable connected, so the platform isn't completely mobile. And once you have begun the program, you can't alter the behavior of your program. In this section, you will use the principles from *Chapter 1, Preparing the BeagleBone Black*, to issue voice commands to initiate movement.

You'll need to modify your voice recognition program so that it can run your Python program when it gets a voice command. You have to make a simple modification to the `continuous.c` program in /home/ubuntu/pocketsphinx-0.8/src/programs. To do this, type `cd /home/ubuntu/ pocketsphinx-0.8/src/programs`, and then type `emacs continuous.c`. The changes will occur in the same section as your other voice commands and will look like this:

```
ubuntu@arm: ~/pocketsphinx-0.8/src/programs
File Edit Options Buffers Tools C Help
        fflush(stdout);
        /* Finish decoding, obtain and print result */
        ps_end_utt(ps);
        hyp = ps_get_hyp(ps, NULL, &uttid);
        printf("%s: %s\n", uttid, hyp);
        fflush(stdout);

        /* Exit if the first word spoken was GOODBYE */
        if (hyp) {
            sscanf(hyp, "%s", word);
            if (strcmp(word, "GOOD BYE") == 0)
                break;
            else if (strcmp(word, "FORWARD") == 0)
                {
                    system("/home/ubuntu/maestro_linux/robot.py");
                    break;
                }
        }

        /* Resume A/D recording for next utterance */
        if (ad_start_rec(ad) < 0)
            E_FATAL("Failed to start recording\n");
    }
-UU-:**--F1   continuous.c   80% L331   (C/1 Abbrev) ---------------------
```

The additions are pretty straightforward. Let's walk through them:

- `else if (strcmp(word, "FORWARD") == 0)`: This checks the word as recognized by your voice command program. If it corresponds with the word `FORWARD`, it will execute everything inside the `if` statement. We use `{ }` to tell the system which commands go with this `else if` clause.

- `system("/home/ubuntu/maestro_linux/robot.py")`: This is the program we will execute. In this case, our mobile platform will do whatever the `robot.py` program tells it to do.

After doing this, you will need to recompile the program, so type `make` and the `pocketSphinx_continuous` executable will be created. Run the program by typing `./pocketSphinx_continuous`. Don't forget the `./` at the start of this command or you'll run a different version of the program. When the program is running, you can disconnect the LAN cable, and the mobile platform will now take the forward voice command and execute your program.

# Summary

You now have a robot than can walk! You can also add other sensors, like the ones you discovered for your tracked robot, sensors that can watch for barriers, or even a webcam.

In the next chapter, you'll start on a new robot. You'll build a robot that can sail under your control or autonomously. You'll start by adding some basic control, then you'll learn how to add a device to sense the wind and a GPS to add direction.

# 6
# A Robot that Can Sail

You've built robots that can navigate on land; now let's look at some amazingly cool possibilities for utilizing the tools to build some robots that dazzle the imagination. You don't want to limit your robotic possibilities to just walking or rolling. You might want your robot to sail. In this chapter, you'll see how to build a robot that can sail the open sea, or at least your local park's pond.

In this chapter, you will build the basic sailing platform. To do this, you will learn the following:

- Using the BeagleBone Black to control servos directly
- Communicating with your platform via long range RF signals so that you can retain control of your robotic sailboat

## The BeagleBone Black and robots that can sail

Now that you've discovered that the BeagleBone Black can guide platforms that can move on land, let's turn to a completely different type of mobile platform, one that can sail. In this section, you'll discover how to add the BeagleBone Black to a sailing platform and utilize it to control your sailboat.

# Building the sailboat platform

Fortunately, sailing in water is about as simple as walking on land. First, however, you need a sailing platform. Here is an image of an RC sailing platform that can be modified to accept control from the BeagleBone Black:

In fact, many RC controller boats can be modified to add the BeagleBone Black. All you need is space to put the processor, the battery, and any additional control circuitry that you might need. In this case, the sailing platform has basically two controls: a rudder that is controlled by a servo and a second servo that controls the position of the sail. These are shown here:

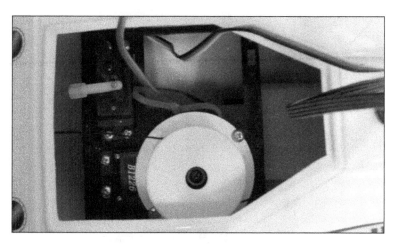

You'll use your BeagleBone Black to control these two servos that will control both the rudder and the sail position, so let's start by connecting these two servos to the BeagleBone Black. You'll drive the two servomotor control signals from the BeagleBone Black GPIO pins, but you'll supply the DC power from a battery.

# Controlling servos with the BeagleBone Black

Once you have assembled your sailboat, you'll want to hook up the BeagleBone Black to the servos on the boat. In order to connect this servomotor to your BeagleBone Black, you'll need some male-to-male jumper cables. You'll notice that there are three wires coming from the servo. Two of these supply the voltage and current to the servo. The third provides a control signal that tells the servo where and how to move.

The best way to connect the servo is to connect the power wires to a battery that will supply power to the servos. The servos will want something more than 6 volts; a 2-cell 7.4 volt LiPo RC battery is an excellent choice. Here is an image of one of these:

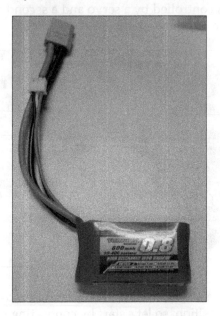

You'll also need a USB battery to supply the BeagleBone Black with power. You can connect the servos to the power of this LiPo battery by using male-to-male solderless wires. The red wire output of the LiPo battery will be 7.4 volts, and the black wire output will be GND. Here is an image of these connections:

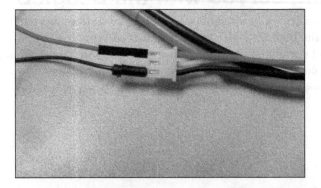

You will connect the control signal of the servos to the GPIO pins of the BeagleBone Black. There are two GPIO pin connectors on the BeagleBone Black, one on each side of the board. They are labeled **P8** and **P9**, but just in case you again need an image with the pin-out, it is here:

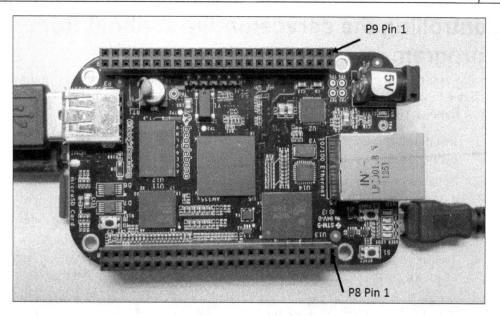

Connect the control wire connection on each servo, normally a yellow wire, to one of the GPIO pins on the BeagleBone Black that supports PWM output. For example, connect P8_13 and P9_14 on the BeagleBone Black. You can use P8_13 and P9_14 for the two servos in this project. Here is an image of the connections:

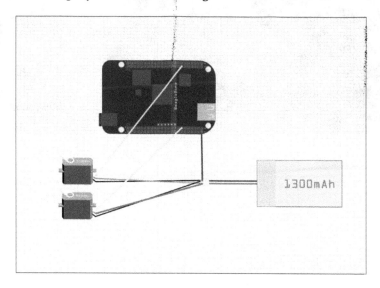

When you have the electrical connections made, you'll need to write some code for the BeagleBone Black.

# Controlling the servos on the sailboat from a program

In order to control the servos with a Python script, if you have not done it previously, you'll need to add a library that will allow you to talk to the GPIO pins via Python. Follow these steps:

1.  Install the `sudo apt-get install build-essential python-dev python-setuptools python-pip python-smbus` packages.

2.  Type `sudo easy_install -U distribute`. This will install `easy_install`, a utility that will help manage Python packages.

3.  Now type `sudo pip install Adafruit_BBIO`. This will install the Adafruit library for talking via the GPIO pins.

4.  To test your installation, type `sudo python -c "import Adafruit_BBIO. GPIO as GPIO; print GPIO"`, and you should see a screen like this:

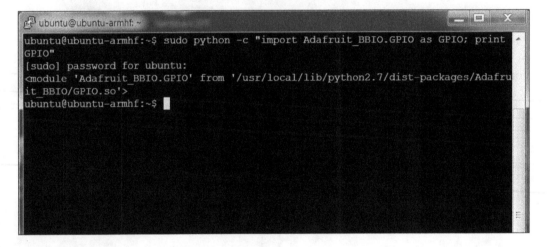

```
ubuntu@ubuntu-armhf: ~
ubuntu@ubuntu-armhf:~$ sudo python -c "import Adafruit_BBIO.GPIO as GPIO; print
GPIO"
[sudo] password for ubuntu:
<module 'Adafruit_BBIO.GPIO' from '/usr/local/lib/python2.7/dist-packages/Adafru
it_BBIO/GPIO.so'>
ubuntu@ubuntu-armhf:~$
```

When you have installed the library, create this program to give you basic control over the two servos:

```
root@arm: /home/ubuntu/sail                                        _  □  X
File Edit Options Buffers Tools Python Help
#!/usr/bin/python
import Adafruit_BBIO.PWM as PWM

servo_pin1= "P8_13"
servo_pin2= "P9_14"
PWM.start(servo_pin1, 95.0, 60.0)
PWM.start(servo_pin2, 95.0, 60.0)

while True:
    servo = int(raw_input("Servo (1 or 2): "))
    angle = raw_input("Angle (0 to 180 x to exit): ")
    if angle == 'x':
        PWM.stop(servo_pin)
        PWM.cleanup()
        break
    angle_f = float(angle)
    duty = angle_f/10;
    if servo == 1:
        PWM.set_duty_cycle(servo_pin1, duty)
    else:
        PWM.set_duty_cycle(servo_pin2, duty)




-UU-:----F1   servo.py       All L2      (Python) ----------------------------
```

When you run the program, you should be able to enter the servo number you wish to control and the desired angle so that the servos can move to that angle. If you need more information on servo control using the BeagleBone Black, look at https://learn.adafruit.com/controlling-a-servo-with-a-beaglebone-black?view=all. Now you can sail your boat, but you'll need to add the ability to talk to it remotely.

# Remote control of the sailboat

To sail the boat, you'll want to be able to send it commands from quite a distance. One possible solution is wireless LAN. Unfortunately, most lakes or ponds won't have an open wireless network available. You could create your own WLAN access point, but the range will still be somewhat limited. The best possible solution is to use **ZigBee** wireless devices to connect your sailboat to a computer.

# A ZigBee tutorial

The ZigBee standard is built upon the IEEE 802.15.4 standard, a standard that was created to allow a set of devices to communicate with each other to enable low data rate coordination of multiple devices. The ZigBee part of the standard ensures interoperability between vendors of these low-rate devices. The IEEE 802.15.4 part of the standard specifies the physical interface and the ZigBee part of the standard defines the network and applications interface. Since we are only interested in the physical interface working together, you can buy IEEE 802.15.4 devices, but ZigBee devices are a bit more prevalent and are a superset of the IEEE 802.15.4 and are also quite inexpensive.

The other standard that you might see as you try to purchase or use devices like these is **XBee**. This is a specific company's implementation, Digi, of several different wireless standards with standard hardware modules that can connect in many different ways to different embedded systems. Their website is available at http://www.digi.com/xbee/. They make some devices that support ZigBee; here is an image of this type of device attached to a shield that provides a USB port:

The advantage of using this device is that it is configured to make it very easy to create and manage a simple link between two XBee series #1 devices. Make sure that you have an XBee device that supports ZigBee series #1. You'll also need to purchase a shield that provides a USB port connection to the device. Note that some USB XBee shields require a special driver to talk to the device; check yours when you purchase the device.

Now, let's get started by configuring your two devices to talk. Plug one of the devices into your personal computer. Your computer should find the latest drivers for the device. You should see your device when you select the **Devices and Printers** section from the Start menu, like this:

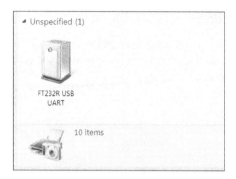

The device is now available to communicate with via the IEEE 802.15.4 wireless interface. We could set up a full ZigBee-compliant network, but we're just going to communicate from one device to another directly, so we'll just use the device as a serial port connection. Double-click on the device, and then select the **Hardware** tab. You should see this:

Note that the device is connected to the **COM20** serial port. We'll use this to communicate with the device and configure it. You can use any terminal emulator program; I like to use PuTTY, which is already on my computer. It is free and available at `http://www.chiark.greenend.org.uk/~sgtatham/putty/download.html`.

Perform the following steps to configure the device:

1. Open PuTTY. Select the **Serial** option and (in this case) the **COM20** port. Here is how to fill in the PuTTY window to do this:

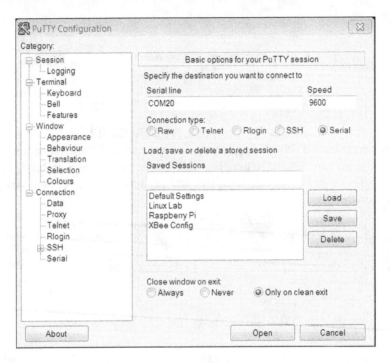

2. Configure the terminal window with the following parameters (the **Serial** option on the **Category** option set): insert 9600 in the **Speed (baud)** field, insert 8 in the **Data bits** field, select **None** from the **Parity** drop-down menu, and insert 1 in the **Stop bits** field.

3. Select the **Terminal** option on the left-hand side of the window. Make sure that you also select **Force On** for **Local Echo,** and check the **Implicit CR in every LF** and **Implicit LF in every CR** checkboxes:

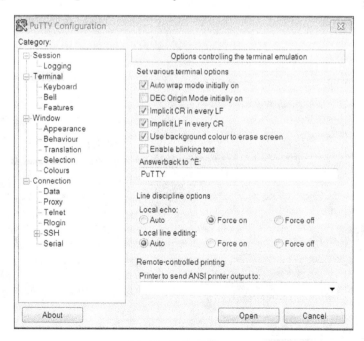

4.  Connect to the device by selecting **Open**.

5.  Enter the following commands in the device through the terminal window:

The **OK** response comes back from the device as you enter each command.
Now plug the other device into the PC. Note that it might choose a different COM port. Go to the **Devices and Printers** section, double-click on the device, and select the **Hardware** tab to find the COM port. Follow the same steps to configure the second device, except that there will be two changes. Here is the terminal window for these commands:

The devices are now ready to talk to each other. Plug one of the devices into the BeagleBone Black USB port. Using a terminal window, show that the devices are connected by typing `ls /dev/tty*`. It will look something like this:

```
ubuntu@arm: ~
login as: ubuntu
ubuntu@10.25.155.175's password:
Welcome to Ubuntu 14.04 LTS (GNU/Linux 3.8.13-bone59 armv7l)

 * Documentation:  https://help.ubuntu.com/
Last login: Wed Jul 23 22:23:56 2014 from grimmettr.c.byui.edu
ubuntu@arm:~$ ls /dev/tty*
/dev/tty      /dev/tty19   /dev/tty3    /dev/tty40   /dev/tty51   /dev/tty62
/dev/tty0     /dev/tty2    /dev/tty30   /dev/tty41   /dev/tty52   /dev/tty63
/dev/tty1     /dev/tty20   /dev/tty31   /dev/tty42   /dev/tty53   /dev/tty7
/dev/tty10    /dev/tty21   /dev/tty32   /dev/tty43   /dev/tty54   /dev/tty8
/dev/tty11    /dev/tty22   /dev/tty33   /dev/tty44   /dev/tty55   /dev/tty9
/dev/tty12    /dev/tty23   /dev/tty34   /dev/tty45   /dev/tty56   /dev/ttyGS0
/dev/tty13    /dev/tty24   /dev/tty35   /dev/tty46   /dev/tty57   /dev/ttyO0
/dev/tty14    /dev/tty25   /dev/tty36   /dev/tty47   /dev/tty58   /dev/ttyS0
/dev/tty15    /dev/tty26   /dev/tty37   /dev/tty48   /dev/tty59   /dev/ttyS1
/dev/tty16    /dev/tty27   /dev/tty38   /dev/tty49   /dev/tty6    /dev/ttyS2
/dev/tty17    /dev/tty28   /dev/tty39   /dev/tty5    /dev/tty60   /dev/ttyS3
/dev/tty18    /dev/tty29   /dev/tty4    /dev/tty50   /dev/tty61   /dev/ttyUSB0
ubuntu@arm:~$ 
```

Notice that the device appears at `/dev/ttyUSB0`. Now you'll need to create a Python program that will read this input. But before you do that, you'll need to download serial communication capability through Python. To do this, type `sudo apt-get install python-serial`. When the download is complete, add your user to the dialout group so that you can use the serial port by typing `sudoadduserubuntudialout`.

Once you have this capability configured, here is a listing of a simple program to communicate via a serial port:

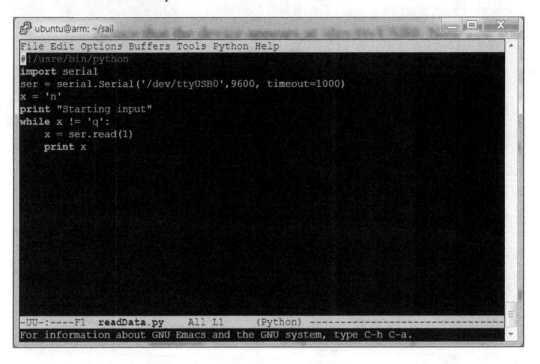

```
ubuntu@arm: ~/sail
File Edit Options Buffers Tools Python Help
#!/usre/bin/python
import serial
ser = serial.Serial('/dev/ttyUSB0',9600, timeout=1000)
x = 'n'
print "Starting input"
while x != 'q':
    x = ser.read(1)
    print x




-UU-:----F1   readData.py     All L1      (Python) -------------------
For information about GNU Emacs and the GNU system, type C-h C-a.
```

Here is what the code does:

- `#!/usr/bin/python`: This allows your program to be executed without invoking Python on the command line.

- `import serial`: This imports the serial port library.

- `Ser = serial.Serial('/dev/ttyUSB0', 9600, timeout = 1000)`: This opens a serial port pointing to the `/dev/ttyUSB1` port, with a baud rate of 9600 and a timeout of 1000 seconds.

- `x = 'n'`: This defines a character variable and initializes it to `'n'`, so we go through the loop at least once.

- `while x != 'q'`: This is a `while` loop; you'll go through this until the user enters the q character.

- `x = ser.read(1)`: This reads one byte from the serial port.

- `print x`: This prints out the value.

Now run `readData.py` in a terminal window on the BeagleBone Black. Run the PuTTY program on your personal computer connected to the other XBee module, but set the flow control to **XON/XOFF**. You should see the characters that you type on the personal computer terminal window comes out on the terminal window running on the BeagleBone Black. Here are the two screens, side by side:

Connecting this functionality to your sailboat is very easy. Start with the `servo.py` program that you created earlier in this chapter. Copy it into a new program by typing `cp servo.py sail.py`. Now let's remove some of the code—parts that you don't need—and add a bit that will accept the character input from the XBee module. Here is a listing of the code:

```python
#!/usr/bin/python
import Adafruit_BBIO.PWM as PWM
import serial

servo_pin1= "P8_13"
servo_pin2= "P9_14"
PWM.start(servo_pin1, 95.0, 60.0)
PWM.start(servo_pin2, 95.0, 60.0)
ser = serial.Serial('/dev/ttyUSB0',9600, timeout=1000)

while True:
    servo = int(ser.read(1))
    print servo
    angle = int(ser.read(3))
    print angle
    angle_f = float(angle)
    duty = angle_f/10;
    if servo == 1:
        PWM.set_duty_cycle(servo_pin1, duty)
    else:
        PWM.set_duty_cycle(servo_pin2, duty)
```

There are really only three changes:

- `import serial`: This imports the serial library.

- `serInput = serial.Serial('/dev/ttyUSB0', 9600, timeout = 1000)`: This line sets up a serial port, getting input from the XBee device. It is important to note that the `USB0` and `USB1` settings might be different in your specific configuration, based on whether the XBee serial device or the motor controller serial device configures first.

- `servo = int(ser.read(1))` and `angle = int(ser.read(3))`: Instead of getting the input from the user via the keyboard, you will be reading the character from the XBee device. The first number will tell which servo you are going to control, 1 or 2; and the next three characters will set the angle to move to, for example, setting the servo to 0 and the angle to 020 would move servo 0 to angle 20.

That's it. Now your sailboat should respond to commands sent from your terminal window on your personal computer. In this case, the first character will determine the servo to move, and the next three will determine the angle for that servo. You could also create an application on the personal computer that could turn mouse movement or some other input into proper commands for your robot.

# Summary

After completing this chapter, you should have a working sailboat where your BeagleBone Black can control the two servos to control the positions of the rudder and the sail. You should also be able to do this remotely at quite a distance using your XBee devices.

In the next chapter, you'll add a GPS device to your sailing platform. That way, you will not only know where you are but can also plan your bearing so that you can sail in an automated way to a new waypoint.

# 7
# Using GPS for Navigation

Your sailboat can sail, but you might want it to sail to a specific location. One of the coolest devices that you can connect to your robot is a GPS location device. It will allow your sailboat to know where it is, and then you can also know the bearing and distance to a new location.

In this chapter, you will be doing the following things:

- Connecting the BeagleBone Black of your sailboat to a GPS device so that it can know where it is

- Accessing the GPS programmatically so that you can use this position to determine the bearing and distance to a new location

## Beginning with a GPS tutorial

Before you get started, let's start with a brief tutorial on GPS. **GPS**, which stands for **Global Positioning System**, is a system of satellites that transmits signals. GPS devices use these signals to calculate a position. There are a total of 24 satellites transmitting signals all around the earth at any given moment, but your device can only *see* the signal from a much smaller set of satellites.

Each of these satellites transmits a very accurate time signal that your device can receive and interpret. It receives the time signal from each of these satellites, and then based on the delay—the time it takes the signal to reach the device—it calculates the position of the receiver based on a procedure called **triangulation**. The following two diagrams illustrate how the device uses the delay differences from three satellites to calculate its position. The system can use more than three satellites, but for the sake of simplicity, let's look at how your device can use three satellites to determine location.

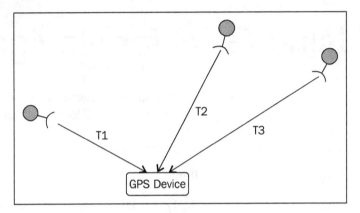

The GPS device receives three signals from **T1**, **T2**, and **T3**, each coded with the time at which the signal was sent. The device then detects three signals. It compares each signal with the current time and determines the time delays associated with receiving these signals. It can then calculate the distance associated with the time the signal took to travel to the device. In the next diagram, the device is at a different location, and the time delays associated with the three signals have changed:

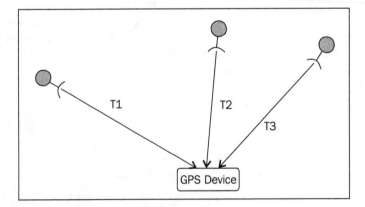

The time delays of the signals **T1**, **T2**, and **T3** can provide the GPS with an absolute position using a mathematical process called triangulation. Since the position of the satellites is known, the amount of time that the signal takes to reach the GPS device is a measure of the distance between that satellite and the GPS device. To simplify, let's show an example in two dimensions. If the GPS device knows the distance from itself to one satellite based on the amount of time delay, we could draw a circle around the satellite at that distance and know that our GPS device is on that sphere, as shown in this diagram:

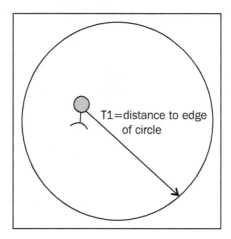

If you have two satellites that send signals and you know the distance between the two, you can draw two circles, as shown in the following diagram:

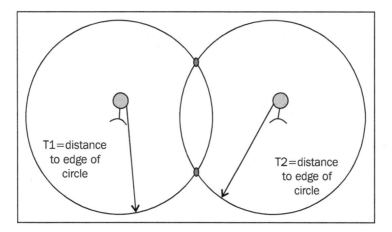

However, you know that since you can only be at points on the circle, you must be at one of the two points that are on both circles. Adding an additional satellite would eliminate one of these two points, providing you with an exact location. You will need more satellites if you are going to do this in all three dimensions. For more information on how GPS works, see http://www.trimble.com/gps_tutorial/.

Now that you know how GPS works, you can connect one to your BeagleBone Black.

# Connecting GPS to the BeagleBone Black

First, you'll need to obtain a GPS unit. There are many that are available, with different interfaces. Connecting a device that has a USB interface is very straightforward. When you plug the USB device into the BeagleBone Black, it will automatically try to recognize the new device and install the driver for it. The advantage of this approach is that it is very easy and you won't need to update any driver files. The problem with this approach is that you will need to add a powered USB hub.

Another possible choice that won't require an additional USB hub is a GPS that can connect to the **RX/TX** GPIO pins of the BeagleBone Black. The VPN1513 GPS Receiver w/ Antenna, marketed by Parallax and available on their online store, is an example of this choice. Here is an image of the device:

You should also purchase an antenna that can connect to the RF (gold) connector on the board. This is type SMA; these are available from electronic online retailers. Here is an image of a possible antenna:

This particular device uses a standard **RX/TX** (UART) interface, one that your BeagleBone Black supports. In order to connect the device, you'll need to connect to the pins on the board. Here is an image of those pins:

You'll connect your BeagleBone Black using the male-to-female solderless jumper cables. Here are the connections on the BeagleBone Black:

| BeagleBone Black pin | GPS cable pin |
| --- | --- |
| P9_3 | VCC |
| P9_1 | GND |
| P9_26 | TX |
| P9_24 | RX |

Now that the two devices are connected, you can access the device via the BeagleBone Black.

# Communicating with the GPS

The GPS device will be talking over the **RX/TX** interface, so you'll need to use the Adafruit libraries that you installed in *Chapter 6, A Robot that Can Sail*. Now you are going to create a simple Python program that will read the location string from your GPS device. Before you do this however, you may need to add some additional software drivers so that your BeagleBone Black can talk via the **RX/TX** interface. To find out if you need to add them, type `ls /dev/tty*` in the prompt. You will be looking for the `/dev/tty01` listing. This will be available in some releases, but in many it will not. If it is not available, then do the following:

1. Go to `www.armhf.com/beaglebone-black-serial-uart-device-tree-overlays-for-ubuntu-and-debian-wheezy-tty01-tty02-tty04-tty05-dtbo-files/` and download the `tty01_armhf.com-00A0.dtbo` file. This is an overlay file that defines a hardware interface. The web page has more information on overlay files, how they are created, and why they are important.

2. Copy this file to the `/lib/firmware` directory.

3. Become the root user by typing `sudo su` and the appropriate passwords.

4. Now you'll need to issue the `echo tty01_armhf.com > /sys/devices/bone_capemgr*/slots` command.

If you've done these steps correctly, you can type in `ls /dev/tty*` and you should now see the `/dev/tty01` device. Unfortunately, you'll need to type the command listed in step 3 and step 4 every time you boot to enable the device. You can type it in a `.*sh` script file to be executed at each startup. See `http://askubuntu.com/questions/814/how-to-run-scripts-on-start-up` for several ways to do this.

Now that your BeagleBone Black can talk via the **RX/TX** interface, you'll create a program to communicate with the GPS unit. To do this, if you are using Emacs as an editor, type `emacs measgps.py`. A new file called `measgps.py` will be created. Then type the following code:

Let's go through the code to see what's happening:

- `#!/usr/bin/python`: As before, the first line simply makes this file available for you to execute from the command line.

- `import Adafruit_BBIO.UART as UART`: You'll import the Adafruit UART library. This will allow us to interface with the BeagleBone Black's GPIO pins.

- `import serial`: This allows you to import the serial library to interface with the **RX/TX** port.

- `UART.setup("UART2")`: This initializes the interface to the `tty01` device.

- `ser = serial.Serial(port = "/dev/tty01", baudrate=9600)`: This command sets up the serial port to use the `/dev/tty01` device, which is our GPS sensor, using a baud rate of 9600.

- `x = ser.read(1200)`: This is the next command that reads a set of values from the **RX/TX** port. In this case, you read 1200 values that will include a full set of GPS data.

- `print x`: This is the final command that prints the value.

- `ser.close()`: This command closes the serial port.

- `UART.clearup()`: This cleans up the UART port.

Once this file has been created, you can run the program and talk to the device. Do this by typing `sudo python measgps.py` and the program will run. You should see something like the following screenshot:

```
ubuntu@ubuntu-armhf:~/gps$ python measgps.py
$GPGGA,160113.167,,,,,0,00,,,M,0.0,M,,0000*52
$GPGLL,,,,,160113.167,V,N*7E
$GPGSA,A,1,,,,,,,,,,,,,,,*1E
$GPRMC,160113.167,V,,,,,,,011013,,,N*4B
$GPVTG,,T,,M,,N,,K,N*2C
$GPGGA,160114.170,,,,,0,00,,,M,0.0,M,,0000*53
$GPGLL,,,,,160114.170,V,N*7F
$GPGSA,A,1,,,,,,,,,,,,,,,*1E
$GPRMC,160114.170,V,,,,,,,011013,,,N*4A
$GPVTG,,T,,M,,N,,K,N*2C
$GPGGA,160115.170,,,,,0,00,,,M,0.0,M,,0000*52
$GPGLL,,,,,160115.170,V,N*7E
$GPGSA,A,1,,,,,,,,,,,,,,,*1E
$GPRMC,160115.170,V,,,,,,,011013,,,N*4B
$GPVTG,,T,,M,,N,,K,N*2C
$GPGGA,160116.167,,,,,0,00,,,M,0.0,M,,0000*57
$GPGLL,,,,,160116.167,V,N*7B
$GPGSA,A,1,,,,,,,,,,,,,,,*1E
$GPGSV,1,1,00*79
$GPRMC,160116.167,V,,,,,,,011013,,,N*4E
$GPVTG,,T,,M,,N,,K,N*2C
$GPGGA,160117.167,,,,,0,00,,,M,0.0,M,,0000*56
$GPGLL,,,,,160117.167,V,N*7A
$GPGSA,A,1,,,,,,,,,,,,,,,*1E
$GPRMC,160117.167,V,,,,,,,011013,,,N*4F
$GPVTG,,T,,M,,N,,K,N*2C
$GPGGA,160118.170,,,,,0,00,,,M,0.0,M,,0000*5F
$GPGLL,,,,,160118.170,V,N*73
$GPGSA,A,1,,,,,,,,,,,,,,,*1E
$GPRMC,160118.170,V,,,,,,,011013,,,N*46
$GPVTG,,T,,M,,N,,K,N*2C
$GPGGA,160119.170,,,,,0,00,,,M,0.0,M,,0000*5E
$GPGLL,,,,,160119.170,V,N*72
$GPGSA,A,1,,,,,,,,,,,,,,,*1E
$GPRMC,160119.170,V,,,,,,,011013,,,N*
ubuntu@ubuntu-armhf:~/gps$
```

The device is providing raw readings back to you, which is a good sign. Unfortunately there isn't much good data here as the unit is inside. How do you know this? Look at one of the lines that start with $GPRMC. This line should tell you your current latitude and longitude values. The GPS is reporting the following command:

```
$GPRMC,160119.170,V,,,,,,,011013,,,N*
```

This line of data should show results similar to the following, with each field separated by a comma:

| | |
|---|---|
| 0 | $GPRMC |
| 1 | 220516 |
| 2 | A |
| 3 | 5133.82 |
| 4 | N |
| 5 | 00042.24 |
| 6 | W |
| 7 | 173.8 |
| 8 | 231.8 |
| 9 | 130694 |
| 10 | 004.2 |
| 11 | W |
| 12 | *70 |

The following is the explanation of each of these fields:

| Field | Value | Explanation |
|---|---|---|
| 1 | 220516 | Timestamp |
| 2 | A | Validity—A (OK), V (Invalid) |
| 3 | 5133.82 | Current latitude |
| 4 | N | North or south |
| 5 | 00042.24 | Current longitude |
| 6 | W | East or west |
| 7 | 173.8 | Speed in knots you are moving |
| 8 | 231.8 | Course—the angle direction in which you are moving |
| 9 | 130694 | Date stamp |
| 10 | 0004.2 | Magnetic variation—variation from magnetic and true North |
| 11 | W | East or West |
| 12 | *70 | Checksum |

In this case, field number 2 reports V, which means the unit cannot find enough satellites to get a position. Taking the unit outside, you should get something like this with your `measgps.py` file:

```
ubuntu@ubuntu-armhf: ~/gps
ubuntu@ubYÆFÆ&ævÆV&æÆÒcÒfæÆÒcÆ¦VVkps.py
$GPGLL,,4349.1422,N,11146.1055,W,020737.000,A,A*47
$GPGSA,A,3,22,21,15,18,,,,,,,,,5.4,2.7,4.7*3B
$GPRMC,020737.000,A,4349.1422,N,11146.1055,W,0.32,289.37,021013,,,A*77
$GPVTG,289.37,T,,M,0.32,N,0.6,K,A*0D
$GPGGA,020738.000,4349.1425,N,11146.1059,W,1,04,2.7,1521.1,M,-16.9,M,,0000*52
$GPGLL,4349.1425,N,11146.1059,W,020738.000,A,A*43
$GPGSA,A,3,22,21,15,18,,,,,,,,,5.4,2.7,4.7*3B
$GPRMC,020738.000,A,4349.1425,N,11146.1059,W,0.75,280.54,021013,,,A*7C
$GPVTG,280.54,T,,M,0.75,N,1.4,K,A*01
$GPGGA,020739.000,4349.1428,N,11146.1066,W,1,04,2.7,1521.0,M,-16.9,M,,0000*53
$GPGLL,4349.1428,N,11146.1066,W,020739.000,A,A*43
$GPGSA,A,3,22,21,15,18,,,,,,,,,5.4,2.7,4.7*3B
$GPRMC,020739.000,A,4349.1428,N,11146.1066,W,1.34,243.86,021013,,,A*78
$GPVTG,243.86,T,,M,1.34,N,2.5,K,A*07
$GPGGA,020740.000,4349.1426,N,11146.1064,W,1,04,2.7,1523.6,M,-16.9,M,,0000*55
$GPGLL,4349.1426,N,11146.1064,W,020740.000,A,A*41
$GPGSA,A,3,22,21,15,18,,,,,,,,,5.4,2.7,4.7*3B
$GPRMC,020740.000,A,4349.1426,N,11146.1064,W,1.82,214.11,021013,,,A*7B
$GPVTG,214.11,T,,M,1.82,N,3.4,K,A*06
$GPGGA,020741.000,4349.1422,N,11146.1068,W,6,00,50.0,1523.3,M,-16.9,M,,0000*6A
$GP
ubuntu@ubuntu-armhf:~/gps$
```

Notice that the `$GPRMC` line now reads this:

`$GPRMC,020740.000,A,4349.1426,N,11146.1064,W,1.82,214.11,021013,,,A*7B`

The field values are now as follows:

| Field | Value | Explanation |
|---|---|---|
| 1 | 020740.000 | Timestamp |
| 2 | A | Validity — A (OK), V (Invalid) |
| 3 | 4349.1426 | Current latitude |
| 4 | N | North or south |
| 5 | 11146.1064 | Current longitude |
| 6 | W | East or west |
| 7 | 1.82 | Speed in knots you are moving |
| 8 | 214.11 | Course — the angle direction in which you are moving |
| 9 | 021013 | Date stamp |
| 10 | | Magnetic variation — variation from magnetic north to true north |

| Field | Value | Explanation |
|-------|-------|-------------|
| 11 |  | East or west |
| 12 | *7B | Checksum |

Now you know where you are. However, it is in the raw form. In the next section, you will learn how to do something with these readings.

# Parsing the GPS information

Your project will now have the GPS connected and also have access to querying the data via serial port. In this section, you will create a program to use this data to find where you are, and then you can determine what to do with that information.

If you have completed the last section, you should be able to receive the raw data from the GPS unit. Now you will be able to take this data and do something with it. For example, you can find your current latitude, longitude, and altitude, and then decide if your goal location is to the east or west, and to the north or south.

The first thing you'll need to do is parse the information out of the raw data. As noted previously, your position and speed are in the $GPMRC output of our GPS. First, you will write a program to simply parse out a couple of pieces of information from that data. Create a new file that looks like this screenshot:

Here are the details of the code shown in the preceding screenshot:

- `#!/usr/bin/python`: As always, the first line simply makes this file available for you to execute from the command line.

- `import serial`: This line allows you to import the serial library to interface with the **RX/TX** port.

- `UART.setup("UART2")`: This initializes the interface to the `tty01` device.

- `ser = serial.Serial(port = "/dev/tty01", baudrate=9600)`: This command sets up the serial port to use the `/dev/tty01` device, which is your GPS sensor, using a baud rate of 9600.

- `x = ser.read(1200)`: This is the next command that reads a set of values from the **RX/TX** port. In this case, you read 1200 values, which will include a full set of GPS data.

- `pos1 = x.find("$GPRMC")`: This will find the first occurrence of `$GPRMC` and set the value of `pos1` to that position. In this case, you want to isolate the `$GPRMC` response line.

- `pos2 = x.find("\n", pos1)`: This will find the `pos1` string variable.

- `loc = x[pos1:pos2]`: The `loc` variable will now hold the line with all the information you are interested in.

- `data = loc.split(',')`: This will take your comma-separated line and break it into an array of values.

- `if data[2] == 'V'`: You now check to see if the data is valid. If not, the next line simply prints that you did not find a valid location.

- `else`: If the data is valid, the next few lines will print the various pieces of data.

Here is a screenshot showing the results when my device was able to find its location:

```
ubuntu@ubuntu-armhf: ~/gps
ubuntu@ubuntu-armhf:~/gps$ python location.py
Latitude = 4349.1418N
Longitude = 11146.1002W
Speed = 1.15
Course = 38.60
ubuntu@ubuntu-armhf:~/gps$
```

Now you have the information about your current location.

# Calculating distance and bearing

Now that you have the data, you can do some interesting things with it. For your sailboat, you'll need to use your current location and a desired new location to give your sailboat a distance and a bearing.

**Longitude** from your GPS device is a measure of where you are on the earth with respect to east/west. **Latitude** is a measure of where you are with respect to north/south. These readings are normally given in degrees (considering the fact that the globe is round, so the readings start at 0 degrees and end at 360 degrees.) Since the earth is very large, the readings also include minutes and seconds, where a single degree is divided into 60 minutes and each minute is divided into 60 seconds.

In order to calculate distance and bearing, you're going to start with longitudinal and latitudinal positions on the earth's surface in the degrees.minutes.seconds format. You'll then translate these values into a digital degree format and use the **haversine formula** to calculate distance and bearing.

To understand the details of how the haversine formula works, refer to http://en.wikipedia.org/wiki/Haversine_formula. The website at http://www.movable-type.co.uk/scripts/latlong.html shows how the formula can be used to calculate distance and bearing.

Here is the Python code that shows the functions that convert the `degree.minutes.seconds` format to the digital degrees format, a function that calculates distance using the haversine formula, and another function to calculate the bearing to a new location:

```python
#!/usr/bin/python
import Adafruit_BBIO.UART as UART
import serial
from math import *

def convert(dms):
  D = int(dms[0:3])
  M = int(dms[3:5])
  S = float(dms[5:])
  DD = D + float(M)/60 + float(S)/3600
  return DD

def distance(lon2, lat2, lon1, lat1):
  radius = 6371 # km
  dlat = radians(lat2-lat1)
  dlon = radians(lon2-lon1)
  a = sin(dlat/2) * sin(dlat/2) + cos(radians(lat1)) * cos(radians(lat2)) * sin(dl\
on/2) * sin(dlon/2)
  c = 2 * atan2(sqrt(a), sqrt(1-a))
  d = radius * c
  return d

def bearing(lat1, lon1, lat2, lon2):
  startLat = radians(lat1)
  startLong = radians(lon1)
  endLat = radians(lat2)
  endLong = radians(lon2)
  dLong = endLong - startLong
  dPhi = log(tan(endLat/2.0+pi/4.0)/tan(startLat/2.0+pi/4.0))
  if abs(dLong) > pi:
    if dLong > 0.0:
        dLong = -(2.0 * pi - dLong)
    else:
        dLong = (2.0 * pi + dLong)
  bearing = (degrees(atan2(dLong, dPhi)) + 360.0) % 360.0;
  return bearing

UART.setup("UART2")
ser = serial.Serial(port = "/dev/ttyO1", baudrate=9600)
```

The following is the code that illustrates how to call these functions:

```
ubuntu@arm: ~/sail
File Edit Options Buffers Tools Python Help
    endLat = radians(lat2)
    endLong = radians(lon2)
    dLong = endLong - startLong
    dPhi = log(tan(endLat/2.0+pi/4.0)/tan(startLat/2.0+pi/4.0))
    if abs(dLong) > pi:
        if dLong > 0.0:
            dLong = -(2.0 * pi - dLong)
        else:
            dLong = (2.0 * pi + dLong)
    bearing = (degrees(atan2(dLong, dPhi)) + 360.0) % 360.0;
    return bearing

UART.setup("UART2")
ser = serial.Serial(port = "/dev/tty01", baudrate=9600)

long1 = "1114813.22"
lat1 = "04346.9905"
desiredLong = convert(long1)
desiredLat = convert(lat1)

x = ser.read(1200)
pos1 = x.find("$GPRMC")
pos2 = x.find("\n", pos1)
loc = x[pos1:pos2]
data = loc.split(',')
if data[2] == 'V':
    print 'No location found'
else:
    lat2 = '0' + data[3] + data[4]
    lat2 = lat2[:-1]
    long2 = data[5] + data[6]
    long2 = long2[:-1]
    currentLat = convert(lat2)
    currentLong = convert(long2)
    print ("Current Latitude = ", currentLat)
    print ("Current Longitude = ", currentLong)
    print "Current Speed = " + data[7]
    print "Current Course = " + data[8]
    distance = distance(-desiredLong, desiredLat, -currentLong, currentLat)
    print ("Distance = ", distance)
    bearing = bearing(currentLat, -currentLong, desiredLat, -desiredLong)
    print ("Bearing = ", bearing)
ser.close()
UART.cleanup()
-UU-:**--F1  location.py     Bot L47    (Python) --------------------------------
```

The first step in the code is to set up the UART to receive the GPS data. Then you'll set the desired new location in terms of its longitude and latitude, each in the deg. min.sec format. Then the program will get the GPS data, and you can extract the latitude and longitude data from it and convert them to the digital degree format, as mentioned earlier. Then you can call both the distance and the bearing functions, and print both the distance and the bearing to the new point.

# Summary

Now your sailboat has the ability to sail using the control of the rudder and the sail. It also has the ability to both know where it is, and calculate the distance and direction of a new waypoint. However, there is one additional capability that you'll need, that is, information about the wind so that you can actually sail your boat. You'll learn that in the next chapter, and you'll have a complete sailing robot.

# 8
# Measuring Wind Speed – Integrating Analog Sensors

Now your sailboat knows where it is, and you can control the rudder and sail; you'll now want to do some actual sailing. But because you don't have an onboard power source, you're going to rely on the wind for your power. To do this, you'll need some way of sensing both the direction as well as the strength of the wind.

In this chapter, you'll learn the following things:

- Connecting an analog wind sensor to the BeagleBone Black
- Using the BeagleBone Black analog-to-digital converter to read the value of the wind speed
- Some of the basics of sailing so that you can sail in almost any direction

# Connecting an analog wind speed sensor

Since you are going to use wind as your power source, you'll need to know both the direction and strength of the wind. You can do this with an analog wind sensor. Here is an image of a wind sensor that is fairly inexpensive, from www.moderndevices.com:

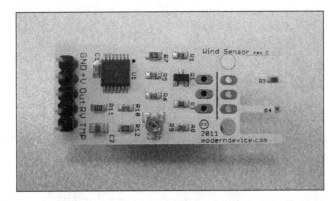

You can mount it to the mast if you'd like. You can perhaps use a small piece of heavy-duty tape and mount it to the top of the mast. However, as you'll see a bit later, it will be useful to be able to turn the sensor in order to do a complete sensing of the wind, so it is useful to mount the sensor to a servo.

In order for the BeagleBone Black to talk with this device, you'll need to connect it to the GPIO pins. Here is a close-up of the connections that the wind sensor requires:

You'll need a **GND** and **+V** connection. The **+V** pin will be connected to the 5-volt connection of the BeagleBone Black, P9_5 of the GPIO set, and the **GND** pin will be connected to the ground connection of the BeagleBone Black ADC, P9_34. The **TMP** pin on this sensor is a temperature measurement—you won't use it in this project.

There are two connections on the wind sensor that you could use to sense wind. The **Out** pin is an output that you can actually calibrate using the small potentiometer on the device. The **RV** pin is the raw voltage output of the sensor. Here is a graph, from the manufacturer's website, of two different outputs at different values temperature and wind speed:

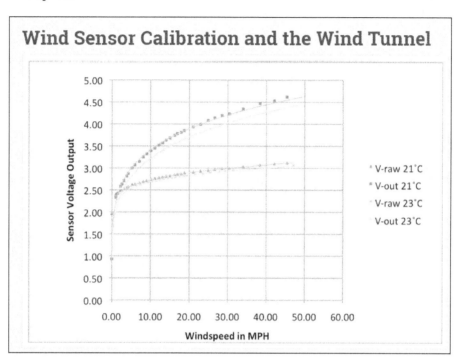

You'll use the **Out** connection, and you'll connect it to one of the ADC inputs on the BeagleBone Black, P9_40. However, you can't connect this input directly to the pin, as the upper limit of the ADC is 1.8 volts, whereas this input can come in at up to 5 volts. You'll need to build a voltage divider circuit to translate the 0- to 5-volt signal to one that has a range from 0 to 1.8 volts, and a calculator to allow you to decide on the resistor values. A voltage divider is a simple circuit that uses two resistors of correct values to scale the voltage. See https://learn.sparkfun.com/tutorials/voltage-dividers for details on the principles behind the voltage divider. In this case, you will need to reduce the voltage by a factor of 1.8/5 or 0.36. If you choose a 1-kilo-ohm resistor for R2, then you'll want a 1.8-kilo-ohm resistor for R1.

Choosing these resistor values also makes sure that the resistors you choose are not so large that the device cannot drive them with enough current for the BeagleBone Black to sense the voltage. They must also not be too small, lest the device drives the BeagleBone Black with too much current. The choices of these two resistor values meets these requirements for this device. Here is a circuit diagram showing how to connect the device using the resistors:

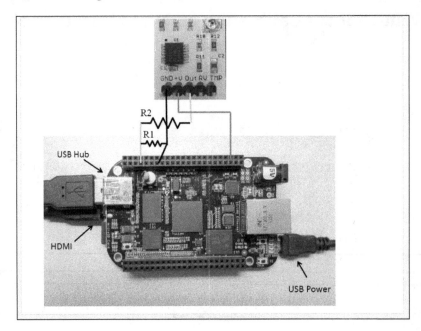

Now that the hardware is connected, you'll want to read the values from the wind sensor programmatically.

# Getting sensor data from the wind speed sensor

You'll use the same Adafruit library that you used in the previous chapters. If you have not installed this library, then install it and follow the instructions in *Chapter 6, A Robot that Can Sail*. Then create the following program:

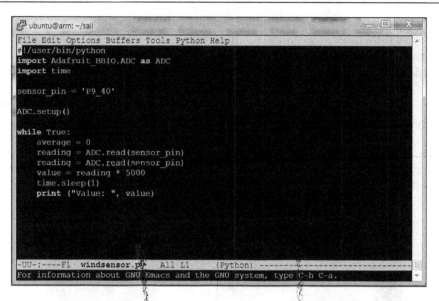

When you run the program, you will see the output of the wind sensor in volts. You can put the wind sensor near a fan and you should see the value change, as shown in the following screenshot:

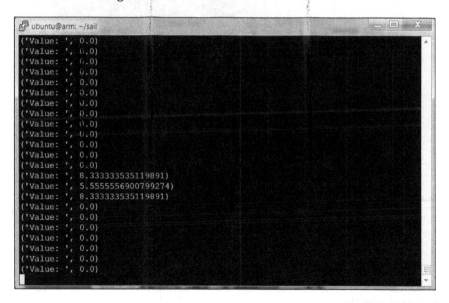

 Note that this will give you an indication of the strength of the wind, but the reading is not calibrated.

In this case, you won't need a calibrated reading but just a relative indication of strength; you'll then use it to gauge the direction of the wind. As noted earlier, you'll want to mount the wind sensor on a servo. This can give you a better indication of the direction of the wind with respect to the sailboat. To do this, connect the servo as noted in *Chapter 6, A Robot that Can Sail*. Connect the control wire connection on this servo to P9_16 on the BeagleBone Black. You had used pins P8_13 and P9_14 for two other servos in this project.

Now you can add the servo control to your `windsensor.py` script to scan and record the strength of the wind with respect to the orientation of your sailboat. Here is a program that does this:

```
ubuntu@arm: ~/sail                                            _  □  X
File Edit Options Buffers Tools Python Help
#!/user/bin/python
import Adafruit_BBIO.ADC as ADC
import Adafruit_BBIO.PWM as PWM
import time

sensor_pin = 'P9_40'
ADC.setup()

servo_pin1= "P9_16"
PWM.start(servo_pin1, 95.0, 60.0)

value=[0.0, 0.0, 0.0, 0.0, 0.0]
while True:
    for i in range(0,5):
        angle = i * 45.0 + 0
        duty = angle/10
        PWM.set_duty_cycle(servo_pin1, duty)
        reading = ADC.read(sensor_pin)
        reading = ADC.read(sensor_pin)
        value[i] = reading * 5000
        time.sleep(1)
        print ("Angle: ", angle, "Value: ", value[i])
    max_value = 0
    max_index = 0
    for i in range(len(value)):
        if max_value < value[i]:
            max_index = i
    print ("Max value at ", max_index * 45.0)

PWM.stop(servo_pin1)
PWM.cleanup()

-UU-:----F1  scanwindsensor.py   All L1    (Python) -------------------
For information about GNU Emacs and the GNU system, type C-h C-a.
```

Most of this code should look familiar. You'll first import the Adafruit libraries that will allow you to access the GPIO pins for the ADC and for the servo control. Then you'll set up the ADC and the servo control. The loop will then go through the angles of 0 degrees, 45 degrees, 90 degrees, 135 degrees, and 180 degrees, giving you the wind sensor reading.

The last section of code simply searches for the maximum value of wind speed at these angles and then returns the angle of the maximum. This will give you the wind direction with respect to the boat's bow.

Here are some sample results of angles and speeds:

```
ubuntu@arm: ~/sail                                          _ □ X
ubuntu@arm:~/sail$ sudo python scanwindsensor.py
('Angle: ',  0.0, 'Value: ', 0.0)
('Angle: ',  45.0, 'Value: ', 0.0)
('Angle: ',  90.0, 'Value: ', 0.0)
('Angle: ',  135.0, 'Value: ', 0.0)
('Angle: ',  180.0, 'Value: ', 0.0)
('Max value at ', 0.0)
('Angle: ',  0.0, 'Value: ', 0.0)
('Angle: ',  45.0, 'Value: ', 2.7777778450399637)
('Angle: ',  90.0, 'Value: ', 5.5555556900799274)
('Angle: ',  135.0, 'Value: ', 0.0)
('Angle: ',  180.0, 'Value: ', 0.0)
('Max value at ', 90.0)
('Angle: ',  0.0, 'Value: ', 0.0)
```

Now you have a way to tell the wind direction.

> One of the challenges of this method is that you will not be able
> to tell the absolute direction of the wind, as the wind sensor won't
> know if it is coming or going. You'll need to use the results of the
> force of the wind on your sailboat to determine whether you are
> sailing with or against the wind.

# Some basics of sailing

Now that you have set up everything, pack up your electronics in any sort of
water-resistant plastic case, and your sailboat should be ready to sail.

> **One word of caution**
> Electronics and water normally do not mix well. Make sure
> that your BeagleBone Black and all the associated circuitry
> is well buttoned up in as watertight a container as possible.
> Use a silicon sealant or some other waterproof sealant from
> where your wires enter or leave the enclosure.

Your sailboat can now sense wind, control the rudder and sail, know where it is and what speed and angle it is moving at, and calculate the bearing and distance to a new destination. In order to complete your robot, you'll need a bit of information on how to sail. First, as a word of caution, this is not coming from an expert sailor, but there are many excellent tutorials on sailing. Try www.simpleeditions.com/61001/how-to-sail for more information on the details of sailing. Also, you'll find a very interesting interactive tutorial on sailing at www.sailx.com.

But, perhaps, some basics are in order. To keep it simple, you need to concern yourself with five things — three inputs and two settings. The first input is the current location, direction, and speed. These will all be available from the GPS unit. The second input is the desired destination location — something that you'll need to program your sailboat to understand. The third input is the wind direction, which will come from the wind sensor.

The first of the two settings is the rudder setting. The rudder is set by controlling the servo attached to it, and it can be straight with the boat, or pointed to the left at some angle, or pointed to the right at an angle. To turn the boat, you will simply set the rudder to the correct position to create a turn. Here is a diagram of the rudder positions for a right and left turn:

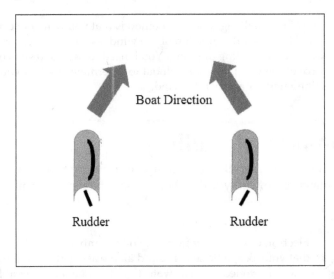

The final setting is the sail setting. This setting can be either in, that is, the sail is pulled tightly so that it is in line with the boat, or out, that is, it can swing out to the side of the boat.

Now let's understand how to sail your boat both with and against the wind. Here is a diagram that will help you understand the concepts of sailing:

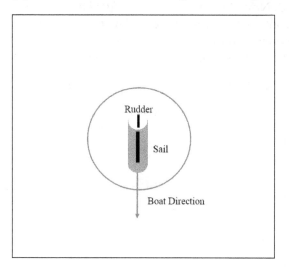

In this case, the diagram shows that the sail is in, and your rudder is in line with the boat. Now let's introduce some wind. If you want to sail with the wind, your boat's rudder and sail should be configured like this:

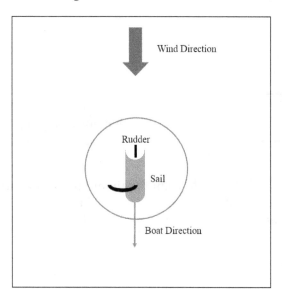

To sail directly with the wind, your rudder should be in line with the boat, but the sail should be all the way out, thus allowing maximum area of the sail to get exposed to the wind. Now it would be wonderful if the wind is always behind your sailboat, but that won't be the case. There will be times when you will want to sail perpendicular to the wind, and even times when you will want to sail against the direction of the wind. So let's look at how to set up your sailboat for these cases.

For the case where you want to sail perpendicular to the wind, you'll need to configure your boat like this:

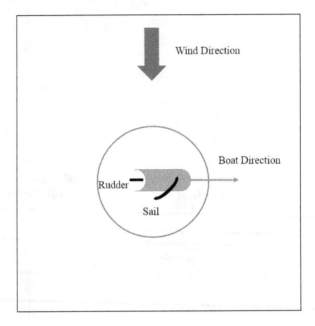

This is called a **beam reach**, and once you have made any turn, you'll adjust your rudder to be straight behind the boat again. The sail will be out at about 45 degrees, or half way between in line with the bow and stern, and all the way to the side.

Now let's cover the case where you want to sail into the wind. First, you need to realize that you cannot sail directly into the wind. This is called **irons**. However, if you point your boat at least 60 degrees from the direction of the wind, you can sail in that direction. Here is a diagram of this orientation:

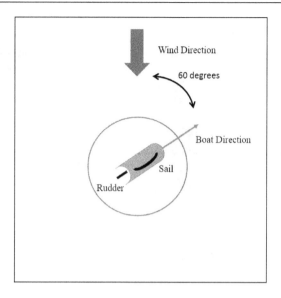

The problem with this is, if you sail in this direction, you cannot reach a destination that is less than 60 degrees in the wind direction. To reach destinations in this area, you'll need to do a manoeuvre called a **tack**. To tack is simply to use a set of manoeuvres, crossing back and forth at a 60 degree angle into the wind, so that you can arrive at a destination that is directly against the direction of the wind. Here is a diagram of tacking:

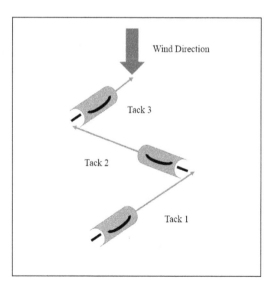

You now have all of the information you need to construct your sailing program.

# Summary

Now you have all the tools to create a program to sail your boat autonomously. It knows where it is and where it is going, and can sense the wind to use that to sail towards a specific destination. The next few chapters will introduce an entirely new application of the BeagleBone Black—and underwater ROV to explore things under the surface of water.

# 9
# An Underwater Remotely
# Operated Vehicle

Now you know how to build a rolling robot, and a sailboat, but what about all the amazing discoveries under the surface of the water? In this chapter, you'll build an underwater **Remotely Operated Vehicle (ROV)**. This will allow you to explore the depths without getting wet.

In this chapter, you'll learn the following:

- Constructing the ROV mechanical system
- Controlling DC motors that can go both ways to power your underwater vehicle

An underwater ROV offers an entirely different way of using the BeagleBone Black to explore a new world. This project is a bit different in two ways. Firstly, there is quite a bit of mechanical work to do, and secondly, it is almost impossible to send wireless signals through water, so you are going to use a tethered control line to give directions to your robot.

## Building the hardware for the ROV

There are several possible approaches to build your ROV. The mechanical design at `openrov.com/page/openrov-2-0` is quite elegant and available for purchase as a complete kit or as component parts. At `openrov.com/page/open-rov-designs-1`, there is a simpler yet similar design. At `www.instructables.com/id/Underwater-ROV/`, there is another design that is very different from the first. All of these designs could certainly use the BeagleBone Black as the embedded controller.

My physical design is based more on the latter design, using mostly plastic PVC piping as shown in the following image:

This hardware design was done using standard PVC for the main chamber and the two chambers that hold the ballast. The main chamber is 12 inches long and 6 inches in diameter. The two smaller chambers are made from two PVC pipes that are 20 inches long and 2 inches in diameter. These small chambers are capped at both ends and hold the weight required to make your ROV neutrally buoyant. Be prepared to add significant weight to your ROV. I had to add 25 pounds of lead to mine to get it to do anything but a bob on top of the surface!

At the rear of the ROV, you'll want some way to be able to gain access to the main chamber while also making it watertight when you want to try your ROV. For this purpose, I used a CHERNE Model # 271578 6-inch Econo-Grip Plug. This is available at most plumbing stores and also online. Here is an image of the CHERNE pipe plug:

The concept of the plug is quite simple. As you tighten the nut, the rubber seal spreads and seals the PVC pipe.

One of the most important components of your ROV is the clear plastic front casing, as you'll need to be able to use a camera to see the world under the water. Here you have two choices. You can go for a flat piece of clear acrylic. Here is an image of the ROV with a flat piece of acrylic:

You can also choose a rounded dome of clear acrylic, as shown in the following image. This came from a company called EZ Tops, and it can be ordered online at `www.eztopsworldwide.com/smalldomes.htm`. You will put it on the end of your ROV, assembled with a gasket and some small bolts. This clear plastic gives you a good view of the underwater world and reduces the drag when moving in the forward direction.

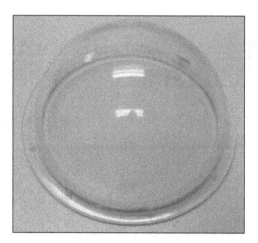

The final piece of hardware that is important is the light. I chose a Cree LED work light, as it is waterproof and provides a significant amount of light while using only 18 watts. It operates from 9 to 12 volts, so I added a 3S RC LiPo battery to power the light.

You'll need three batteries for your project. One 3S RC LiPo battery to power the DC brushless motors, another 3S RC LiPo battery to power the LED light, and a 5 V battery to power the BeagleBone Black. I like to use a simple cell phone charge battery. Here is an image of such a battery:

The motor mounts and offsets are 3D printed in my model, but they can just as easily be constructed out of PVC material available at the local hardware store. The connections between the three PVC parts are made by long bolts inside aluminum rods.

 Make sure you use either rubber washers or silicon caulking at every hole in the main compartment to ensure you don't have any water leaks.

# Controlling brushless DC motors using the BeagleBone Black

Whichever physical design you choose, you'll need to control the motors, and the BeagleBone Black can do this task. In this case, I chose fairly standard brushless DC motors, four Turnigy D2836 9 950KV Brushless Outrunner Motors available at `hobbyking.com`, and then fitted them with RC boat propellers, the Traxxas Propeller Left 4.0mm Villain EX TRA1584 available at `rcplanet.com`. These motors work just fine when underwater and are easy to control with radio-controlled **Electronic Speed Controllers (ESC)**.

For this project, you'll need four brushless DC motors, and four ESC controllers. You'll need to make sure that the ESCs will be able to control the motors to go both forward and backwards. Here is an image of one such unit:

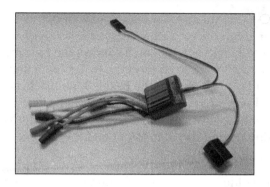

This particular unit is a Turnigy Trackstart 25A ESC, made normally for an RC car, and is available at many retail and online RC outlets. The connections on this unit are straightforward. The red and black wires with plugs go to an RC battery, in this case, a 3S 11.1 volt LiPo RC battery. The other three connections go to the motor. This particular ESC comes with a switch—you won't use it in this particular project. The last connection is a three wire connector similar to a servo connection. You'll connect this to the BeagleBone Black. Here is an image of the connections:

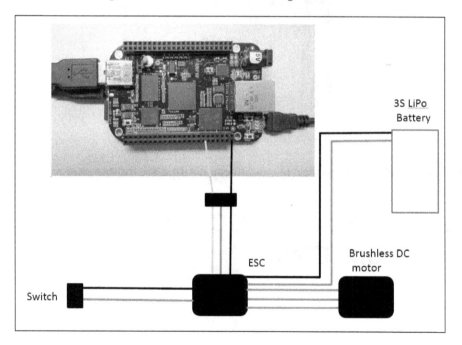

For details on the ESC-to-brushless-DC-motor connection, check the ESC documentation at `http://www.hobbyking.com/hobbyking/store/uploads/981860436X852229X19.pdf`. You'll connect the four motors to the BeagleBone Black, but you'll want to connect the two motors that are pointing forward to two different control pins on the BeagleBone Black, in this case, P8_13 and P9_14. This will allow you to use these two motors to steer the ROV, as you can then move these motors forward and backward separately. You'll connect the motors that are pointing up and down to P9_21 and P9_42.

In order to make this arrangement sturdy, I added a prototyping cape to the BeagleBone Black and solder connectors to facilitate the connections. These bare capes are available online at most retailers that sell the BeagleBone Black. Here is an image of the cape connected to the BeagleBone Black:

Now the connections are available, so you can control the motors programmatically.

# Program to control DC motors using the BeagleBone Black

Now that you've connected your motor, here is a simple Python program to control one of the motors:

```
ubuntu@arm: ~/rov                                          _  □  X
File Edit Options Buffers Tools Python Help
#!/usr/bin/python

import Adafruit_BBIO.PWM as PWM

motor1 = "P8_13"
duty_stop = 9
duty_forward = 12 # 12 max
duty_back = 6      # 6 min
PWM.start(motor1, duty_stop, 60.0)

print "Ready"

key = '0'
while key != 'q':
    key = raw_input(">")
    print key
    if key == '1':              # Forward
       PWM.set_duty_cycle(motor1, duty_forward)
    elif key == '2':        # Backward
       PWM.set_duty_cycle(motor1, duty_back)
    elif key == '3':        # Stop
       PWM.set_duty_cycle(motor1, duty_stop)
    elif key == '4':     # Shutdown
       PWM.stop(motor1)

PWM.cleanup() # stop all signals

-UU-:----F1  simple.py      All L23     (Python) ------------------
Wrote /home/ubuntu/rov/simple.py
```

Let's look at the details. Here are the individual command statements:

- `#!/usr/bin/python`: As noted earlier, this command sets up the program to be executed without invoking Python

- `import Adafruit_BBIO.PWM as PWM`: This library is used to communicate with the GPIO pins

- `motor1 = "P8_13"`: This sets the motor to PWM control P8_13 — the 13th pin on the 8th connector

- `duty_stop = 9`: This sets the duty cycle of the PWM that is needed to stop the motor

- `duty_forward = 12 # 12 max`: This sets the duty cycle of the PWM signal on the control pin that is needed to make the motor go in the forward direction at the maximum speed

- `duty_back = 6       # 6 min`: This sets the duty cycle of the PWM signal on the control pin that is needed to make the motor go in the backward direction at the maximum speed

- `PWM.start(motor1, duty_stop, 60.0)`: This sets the PWM signal to stop the motor before you start the program

- `print "Ready"`: This prints `Ready` to the screen

- `key = '0'`: This initializes the key to be a character with a value of `'0'`

- `while key != 'q'`: This keeps the loop going until `'q'` is entered

- `key = raw_input(">")`: This gets a single character and uses the `'>'` character as a prompt

- `print key`: This prints the character entered

- `if key == '1':          # Forward`: If the key is a 1, then you'll set the motor to go forward

- `PWM.set_duty_cycle(motor1, duty_forward)`: This sets the PWM signal to full power forward

- `elif key == '2':        # Backward` – If the key is a 2, then you'll set the motor to go backward

- `PWM.set_duty_cycle(motor1, duty_back)`: This sets the PWM signal to full power backward

- `elif key == '3':        # Stop`: If the key is 3, then you'll set the motor to stop

- `PWM.set_duty_cycle(motor1, duty_stop)`: This sets the PWM signal to stop

- `elif key == '4':      # Shutdown`: If the key is 4, then this shuts the motor down

- `PWM.stop(motor1)`: This disables the control signal connected to motor1

- `PWM.cleanup() # stop all signals`: This cleans up all the control signals throughout the library

Running this program should cause motor1, which is connected to the P8_13 GPIO pin, to run forward, backward, and stop. You can check all four motors using this code by changing the `motor1 = "P8_13"` statement and placing P9_21, P9_14, or P9_42 inside the quotes. This will allow you to check the state of all four motors.

Controlling the speed and direction of each of these motors will allow you to move your ROV forward, backward, up, and down, as well as turn your ROV. How much speed you would apply will depend on both the size of your ROV and the size of your motors.

The next program controls all the four motors using the keyboard. The following image shows the first part of this program, with the functions to control the motors for the different directions:

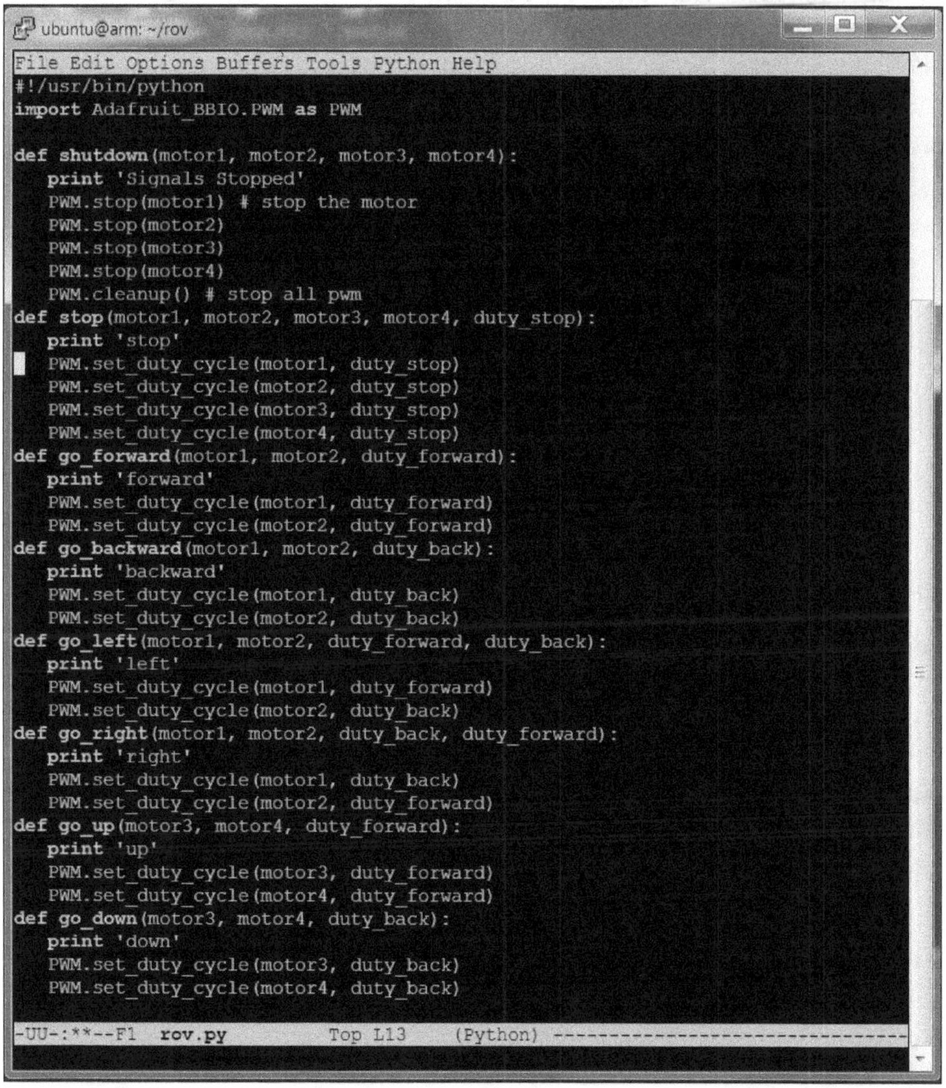

```
ubuntu@arm: ~/rov
File Edit Options Buffers Tools Python Help
#!/usr/bin/python
import Adafruit_BBIO.PWM as PWM

def shutdown(motor1, motor2, motor3, motor4):
   print 'Signals Stopped'
   PWM.stop(motor1) # stop the motor
   PWM.stop(motor2)
   PWM.stop(motor3)
   PWM.stop(motor4)
   PWM.cleanup() # stop all pwm
def stop(motor1, motor2, motor3, motor4, duty_stop):
   print 'stop'
   PWM.set_duty_cycle(motor1, duty_stop)
   PWM.set_duty_cycle(motor2, duty_stop)
   PWM.set_duty_cycle(motor3, duty_stop)
   PWM.set_duty_cycle(motor4, duty_stop)
def go_forward(motor1, motor2, duty_forward):
   print 'forward'
   PWM.set_duty_cycle(motor1, duty_forward)
   PWM.set_duty_cycle(motor2, duty_forward)
def go_backward(motor1, motor2, duty_back):
   print 'backward'
   PWM.set_duty_cycle(motor1, duty_back)
   PWM.set_duty_cycle(motor2, duty_back)
def go_left(motor1, motor2, duty_forward, duty_back):
   print 'left'
   PWM.set_duty_cycle(motor1, duty_forward)
   PWM.set_duty_cycle(motor2, duty_back)
def go_right(motor1, motor2, duty_back, duty_forward):
   print 'right'
   PWM.set_duty_cycle(motor1, duty_back)
   PWM.set_duty_cycle(motor2, duty_forward)
def go_up(motor3, motor4, duty_forward):
   print 'up'
   PWM.set_duty_cycle(motor3, duty_forward)
   PWM.set_duty_cycle(motor4, duty_forward)
def go_down(motor3, motor4, duty_back):
   print 'down'
   PWM.set_duty_cycle(motor3, duty_back)
   PWM.set_duty_cycle(motor4, duty_back)

-UU-:**--F1  rov.py        Top L13     (Python) --------------------------------
```

There are eight functions in the preceding piece of code. They are described as follows:

- `shutdown`: This function disconnects all the GPIO pins from the control library. It also closes the library.
- `stop`: This function stops all the motors.
- `go_forward`: This function puts motor1 and motor2 in the forward full speed state, causing the ROV to move forward.
- `go_backward`: This function puts motor1 and motor2 in the backward full speed state, causing the ROV to move backward.
- `go_left`: This function puts motor1 in the forward full speed state and motor2 in the backward full speed state, causing the ROV to turn left.
- `go_right`: This function puts motor1 in the backward full speed state and motor2 in the forward full speed state, causing the ROV to turn right.
- `go_up`: This function puts motor3 and motor4 in the forward full speed state, causing the ROV to go up.
- `go_down`: This function puts motor3 and motor4 in the full backward speed state, causing the ROV to go down.

The second part of this program is shown here:

```
ubuntu@arm: ~/rov
File Edit Options Buffers Tools Python Help
    PWM.set_duty_cycle(motor4, duty_forward)
def go_down(motor3, motor4, duty_back):
    print 'down'
    PWM.set_duty_cycle(motor3, duty_back)
    PWM.set_duty_cycle(motor4, duty_back)

motor1 = "P8_13"
motor2 = "P9_14"
motor3 = "P9_42"
motor4 = "P9_21"
duty_stop = 9
duty_forward = 12 # 12 max
duty_back = 6       # 6 min
PWM.start(motor1, duty_stop, 60.0)
PWM.start(motor2, duty_stop, 60.0)
PWM.start(motor3, duty_stop, 60.0)
PWM.start(motor4, duty_stop, 60.0)
print "Ready"

key = '0'
while key != 'q':
    key = raw_input(">")
    if key == '1':          # Forward  - Up key
        go_forward(motor1, motor2, duty_forward)
    elif key == '2':        # Backward - Down key
        go_backward(motor1, motor2, duty_back)
    elif key == '3':        # Left     - Left key
        go_left(motor1, motor2, duty_forward, duty_back)
    elif key == '4':        # Right    - Right key
        go_right(motor1, motor2, duty_back, duty_forward)
    elif key == '5':    # UP       - Shift L
        go_up(motor3, motor4, duty_forward)
    elif key == '6':  # Down      - Control L
        go_down(motor3, motor4, duty_back)
    elif key == '7':        # Stop     - space
        stop(motor1, motor2, motor3, motor4, duty_stop)
    elif key == "8":        # Shutdown - Escape
        shutdown(motor1, motor2, motor3, motor4)

PWM.cleanup() # stop all signals
-UU-:**--F1   rov.py          Bot L56    (Python) -----------------------------
```

The preceding part of the code first initializes all four motors, puts them all in the stopped state, then enters a while loop, taking an input from the user, and then responds by moving the ROV in the programmed way.

You might want a more intuitive interface on your project. The next program uses the concepts you have learned, wraps the definitions in the previous program into a class to make them easier to access, and adds a graphical user interface. To get the graphical user interface to work, you'll need to add a graphics capability called `Tkinter`. I won't go into the details on using this; for a good tutorial, go to `zetcode.com/gui/tkinter/`. You get this graphical user interface by typing `sudo apt-get install python-tk`.

Once you have that installed the graphical user interface, you'll need to add the program. Here is the first part of the program, with the Adafruit and Tkinter includes and the first part of the motor class that has all the capabilities in the previous program:

```python
#!/usr/bin/python

import Adafruit_BBIO.PWM as PWM
from Tkinter import *

""" Motor class to control the PWM signals """
class Motor:
    # pwm at P8_13, P9_14, and P9_16, P9_21, P9_42
    motor1 = "P8_13"
    motor2 = "P9_14"
    motor3 = "P9_42"
    motor4 = "p9_21"
    duty_stop = 9
    duty_forward = 12 # 12 max
    duty_back = 6      # 6 min

    def __init__(self):
        """ get everything going """
        # (motor, duty, frequency, polarity)
        print 'Signals Started'
        PWM.start(Motor.motor1, Motor.duty_stop, 60.0)
        PWM.start(Motor.motor2, Motor.duty_stop, 60.0)
        PWM.start(Motor.motor3, Motor.duty_stop, 60.0)
        PWM.start(Motor.motor4, Motor.duty_stop, 60.0)

    def shutdown(self):
        """ stop motors and PWM signals """
        print 'Signals Stopped'
        PWM.stop(Motor.motor1) # stop the motor
        PWM.stop(Motor.motor2)
        PWM.stop(Motor.motor3)
        PWM.stop(Motor.motor4)
        PWM.cleanup() # stop all pwm

    def stop(self):
        """ stop the motors but not the signals """
        print 'stop'
        PWM.set_duty_cycle(Motor.motor1, Motor.duty_stop)
        PWM.set_duty_cycle(Motor.motor2, Motor.duty_stop)
        PWM.set_duty_cycle(Motor.motor3, Motor.duty_stop)
        PWM.set_duty_cycle(Motor.motor4, Motor.duty_stop)
```

```
-UU-:----F1  guirov.py      Top L1      (Python) --------------------------------
For information about GNU Emacs and the GNU system, type C-h C-a.
```

The following screenshot shows the rest of the motor control class that includes the functions for direction control:

```
def go_forward(self):
    self.stop()
    print 'forward'
    PWM.set_duty_cycle(Motor.motor1, Motor.duty_forward)
    PWM.set_duty_cycle(Motor.motor2, Motor.duty_forward)

def go_backward(self):
    self.stop()
    print 'backward'
    PWM.set_duty_cycle(Motor.motor1, Motor.duty_back)
    PWM.set_duty_cycle(Motor.motor2, Motor.duty_back)

def go_left(self):
    self.stop()
    print 'left'
    PWM.set_duty_cycle(Motor.motor1, Motor.duty_forward)
    PWM.set_duty_cycle(Motor.motor2, Motor.duty_back)

def go_right(self):
    self.stop()
    print 'right'
    PWM.set_duty_cycle(Motor.motor1, Motor.duty_back)
    PWM.set_duty_cycle(Motor.motor2, Motor.duty_forward)

def go_up(self):
    self.stop()
    print 'up'
    PWM.set_duty_cycle(Motor.motor3, Motor.duty_forward)
    PWM.set_duty_cycle(Motor.motor4, Motor.duty_forward)

def go_down(self):
    self.stop()
    print 'down'
    PWM.set_duty_cycle(Motor.motor3, Motor.duty_back)
    PWM.set_duty_cycle(Motor.motor4, Motor.duty_back)
```

```
-UU-:----F1  guirov.py      24% L68      (Python) ---------------------------
```

The following is a screenshot that shows the initialization and widget function of a class to create the graphics for your program:

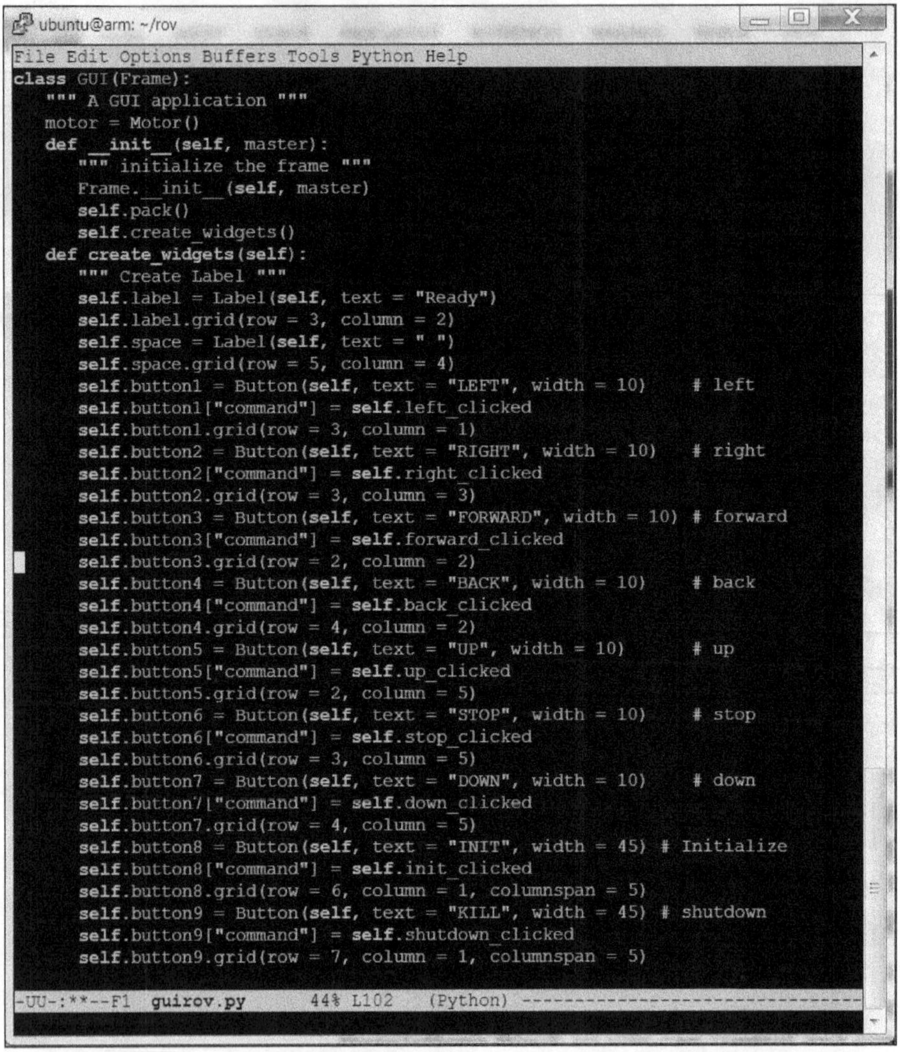

```
ubuntu@arm: ~/rov
File Edit Options Buffers Tools Python Help
class GUI(Frame):
    """ A GUI application """
    motor = Motor()
    def __init__(self, master):
        """ initialize the frame """
        Frame.__init__(self, master)
        self.pack()
        self.create_widgets()
    def create_widgets(self):
        """ Create Label """
        self.label = Label(self, text = "Ready")
        self.label.grid(row = 3, column = 2)
        self.space = Label(self, text = " ")
        self.space.grid(row = 5, column = 4)
        self.button1 = Button(self, text = "LEFT", width = 10)       # left
        self.button1["command"] = self.left_clicked
        self.button1.grid(row = 3, column = 1)
        self.button2 = Button(self, text = "RIGHT", width = 10)      # right
        self.button2["command"] = self.right_clicked
        self.button2.grid(row = 3, column = 3)
        self.button3 = Button(self, text = "FORWARD", width = 10)    # forward
        self.button3["command"] = self.forward_clicked
        self.button3.grid(row = 2, column = 2)
        self.button4 = Button(self, text = "BACK", width = 10)       # back
        self.button4["command"] = self.back_clicked
        self.button4.grid(row = 4, column = 2)
        self.button5 = Button(self, text = "UP", width = 10)         # up
        self.button5["command"] = self.up_clicked
        self.button5.grid(row = 2, column = 5)
        self.button6 = Button(self, text = "STOP", width = 10)       # stop
        self.button6["command"] = self.stop_clicked
        self.button6.grid(row = 3, column = 5)
        self.button7 = Button(self, text = "DOWN", width = 10)       # down
        self.button7["command"] = self.down_clicked
        self.button7.grid(row = 4, column = 5)
        self.button8 = Button(self, text = "INIT", width = 45)  # Initialize
        self.button8["command"] = self.init_clicked
        self.button8.grid(row = 6, column = 1, columnspan = 5)
        self.button9 = Button(self, text = "KILL", width = 45)  # shutdown
        self.button9["command"] = self.shutdown_clicked
        self.button9.grid(row = 7, column = 1, columnspan = 5)
-UU-:**--F1  guirov.py      44% L102    (Python) ---------------------------
```

These functions create the different buttons that will populate your user interface. The next part of this class connects these buttons to the functions of your motor class, as shown in the following screenshot:

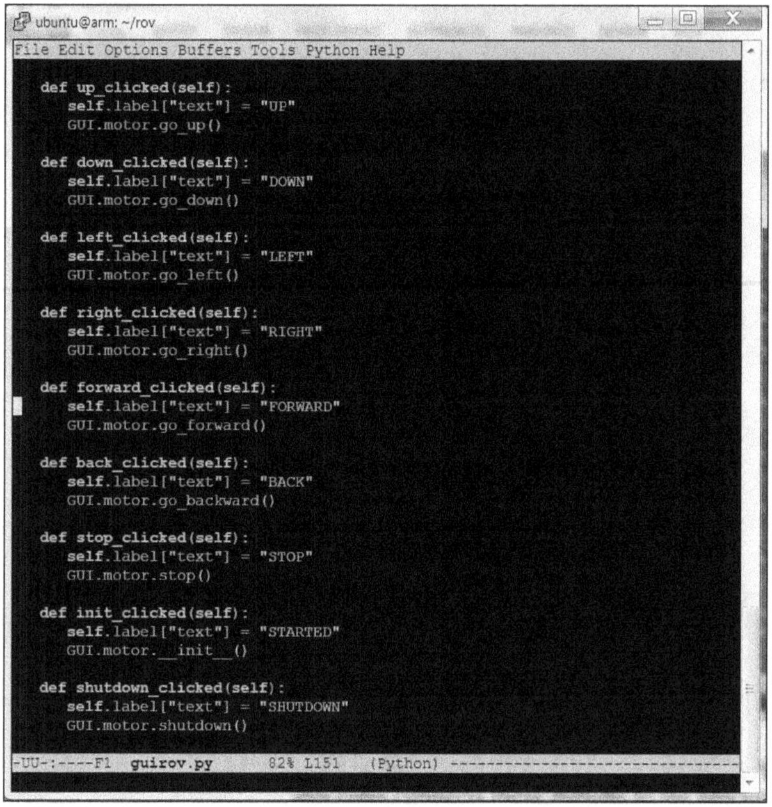

```
ubuntu@arm: ~/rov
File Edit Options Buffers Tools Python Help

    def up_clicked(self):
        self.label["text"] = "UP"
        GUI.motor.go_up()

    def down_clicked(self):
        self.label["text"] = "DOWN"
        GUI.motor.go_down()

    def left_clicked(self):
        self.label["text"] = "LEFT"
        GUI.motor.go_left()

    def right_clicked(self):
        self.label["text"] = "RIGHT"
        GUI.motor.go_right()

    def forward_clicked(self):
        self.label["text"] = "FORWARD"
        GUI.motor.go_forward()

    def back_clicked(self):
        self.label["text"] = "BACK"
        GUI.motor.go_backward()

    def stop_clicked(self):
        self.label["text"] = "STOP"
        GUI.motor.stop()

    def init_clicked(self):
        self.label["text"] = "STARTED"
        GUI.motor.__init__()

    def shutdown_clicked(self):
        self.label["text"] = "SHUTDOWN"
        GUI.motor.shutdown()

-UU-:----F1  guirov.py      82% L151    (Python) ----------------------
```

Finally, the small piece of code that sets up and runs the graphics is in the following screenshot:

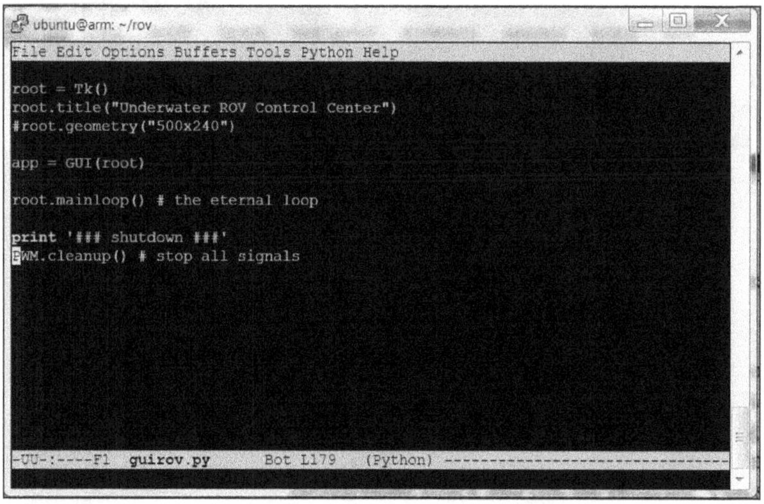

```
ubuntu@arm: ~/rov
File Edit Options Buffers Tools Python Help

root = Tk()
root.title("Underwater ROV Control Center")
#root.geometry("500x240")

app = GUI(root)

root.mainloop() # the eternal loop

print '### shutdown ###'
GWM.cleanup() # stop all signals




-UU-:----F1  guirov.py      Bot L179    (Python) ----------------------
```

You'll need to use the VNC viewer capability you installed in *Chapter 1, Preparing the BeagleBone Black*, to run this graphical program. So start the VNC server by typing `vncserver` in a terminal window on the BeagleBone Black, then go to your host computer and start a VNC viewer. Open a terminal window in the VNC viewer on the BeagleBone Black and run the program. You should get something like this:

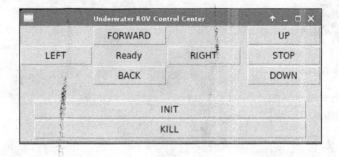

Now your ROV is maneuverable. To complete your ROV project, you'll need two additional capabilities. The first is a long LAN connection from the surface to your BeagleBone Black so that you can control and communicate with your ROV via this LAN cable. The second is a method of seeing underwater. Let's tackle the control problem first.

# Connecting to the BeagleBone Black via a long LAN

The ROV will be controlled from a computer on the service through a very long LAN cable. Fortunately, long LAN cables are readily available at most online electronic stores. I used a 100-foot cable for my ROV. You'll also need to be careful how you pass the LAN cable through the main compartment. I used a 90° Snap Elbow Dome Connector to pass the LAN cable to the main compartment. Here is an image of this part:

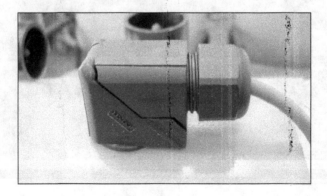

I also found it useful to purchase a hose spool from the local hardware store to organize my LAN cable. The following is an image of a hose spool:

Now you'll need to connect your LAN cable to a computer on the surface so that you can control your ROV. Since the default setting for the BeagleBone Black is to DHCP—a dynamic IP address allocation process—if you want to talk without changing anything, then you'll need a wired router to connect your BeagleBone Black to your computer. This router will help in providing the BeagleBone Black its address. These routers are very inexpensive and available at most electronics stores. Here is an image of a router:

This does require power, which might be difficult if you want to take your monitoring station on the water. If you want to connect the BeagleBone Black to the computer, you'll want to establish a static IP address on the BeagleBone Black. To do this, follow these steps:

1. Issue the following command in a terminal window: `cat /etc/network/interfaces`. You should see something like this:

```
ubuntu@arm: ~/examples/python
auto eth0
iface eth0 inet dhcp
# Example to keep MAC address between reboots
#hwaddress ether DE:AD:BE:EF:CA:FE

# The secondary network interface
#auto eth1
#iface eth1 inet dhcp

# WiFi Example
#auto wlan0
#iface wlan0 inet dhcp
#     wpa-ssid "essid"
#     wpa-psk  "password"

# Ethernet/RNDIS gadget (g_ether)
# ... or on host side, usbnet and random hwaddr
# Note on some boards, usb0 is automaticly setup with an init script
iface usb0 inet static
    address 192.168.7.2
    netmask 255.255.255.0
    network 192.168.7.0
    gateway 192.168.7.1
ubuntu@arm:~/examples/python$ 
```

2. The line that reads `iface eth0 inet dhcp` tells you that the DHCP access is going to try and get a dynamic IP address. You'll need to change this line to `iface eth0 inet static` by editing the file with Emacs.

3. Edit the file and set the desired static address by editing the lines that read:

```
iface usb0 inet static
    address 192.168.7.2
    netmask 255.255.255.0
    network 192.168.7.0
    gateway 192.168.7.1
```

4. Now reboot the BeagleBone Black.

For more details on dynamic and static IP allocation and the BeagleBone Black, go to www.mathworks.com/help/simulink/ug/getting-the-beagleboard-ip-address.html.

That's it! Connect your laptop or a portable computer and you can use the address defined at the bottom of the /etc/network/interfaces file to access the BeagleBone Black wirelessly via an SSH connection or VNC server and control your ROV.

# Accessing a camera for your project

Now that you have established a connection via a long LAN cable, the second capability you'll need is to access a camera to see where you are going. You've already done this as a part of *Chapter 4, Vision and Image Processing*. You can create a simple display window for OpenCV using the camera.py demo program that comes with the open source code. Depending on the camera, you might want to change the resolution of the image. Here is the program that works with the Logitech C270 webcam:

```
#!/usr/bin/python

import cv2.cv as cv
import time

cv.NamedWindow("camera", 1)

capture = cv.CaptureFromCAM(0)
cv.SetCaptureProperty(capture, 3, 360)
cv.SetCaptureProperty(capture, 4, 240)

while True:
    img = cv.QueryFrame(capture)
    cv.ShowImage("camera", img)
    if cv.WaitKey(10) == 27:
        break
cv.DestroyAllWindows()
```

Now that you have these two applications, you'll want to run both the GUI and the camera program so that you can see where you are going and control your ROV. Do this by again using the VNC server capability. In your VNC viewer window, you can run both the programs, and you should see something like this:

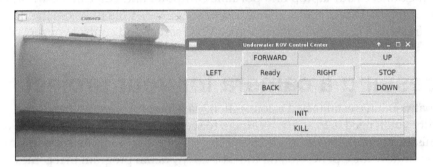

With the image on the left and the controls on the right, you can now control your ROV and explore the underwater world. Mount your camera to the front of the ROV. I used a 3D printed part to mount mine. Then mount your BeagleBone Black into the ROV. I used Velcro to mount it on top of the main compartment. Connect the batteries to the BeagleBone Black, motor controllers, and LED light. Then close your main chamber using the expandable 6-inch plug. You are ready to explore!

This project will require lots of practical tweaking in the water. You'll need to adjust your ballast to make sure your ROV is neutrally buoyant. You'll also have to constantly monitor the watertight nature of your design.

# Summary

In this chapter, you tackled a robot that can go under the water. You learned how to control a project via a LAN connection across a significant distance with the ROV project. In the next chapter, you will move to projects that can fly.

# 10
# A Quadcopter

You've built robots that can roll, walk, sail, and even go under the water. In this chapter, you'll build a robot that can fly. This project will guide you through the process of creating your own quadcopter based on the BeagleBone Black.

In this chapter, we will learn the following:

- Building a quadcopter
- Connecting the BeagleBone Black to the quadcopter
- Controlling the quadcopter using the BeagleBone Black

## Basics of quadcopter flight

Now you'll build robots that can fly by relying on the BeagleBone Black to control their flight. There are several possible ways to incorporate the BeagleBone Black into a flying robotic project; in this case, a quadcopter.

**Quadcopters** are unique flying platforms that have become popular in the last few years. They are flying platforms that utilize the same vertical lift concept as helicopters. However, they employ not one but four motor/propeller combinations to provide an enhanced level of stability. Here is an image of such a platform:

The quadcopter has two sets of counter-rotating propellers, which simply means that two of the propellers rotate one way and the other two rotate the other way to provide thrust in the same direction. This provides a platform that is inherently stable. By controlling the thrust, all the four motors allow you to change pitch, roll, and yaw the device. Here is a diagram that might be helpful:

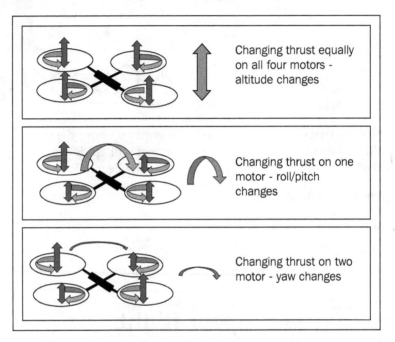

As you can see, controlling the relative speed of the four motors allows you to control the various ways the device can change its position. To move forward, you would want to adjust the pitch so that the quadcopter is tilting forward. Then you'll add some thrust so that instead of going up, the device would move forward, as shown in this diagram:

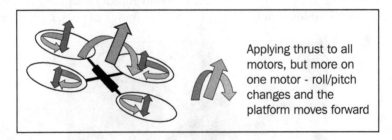

In a perfect world, you might know the components you have used to build a quadcopter and how much control signal to apply to get a certain change in the roll, pitch, yaw, or altitude of the quadcopter. But there are simply too many aspects of your device that can vary to control this directly. Instead, this platform uses a series of measurements of its position—pitch, roll, yaw, and altitude—and then adjusts the control signals to the motors to achieve the desired result. This is called **feedback control**. Here is a diagram of a feedback system:

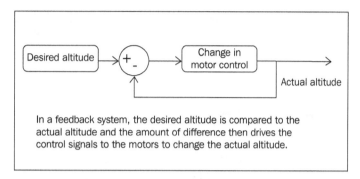

In a feedback system, the desired altitude is compared to the actual altitude and the amount of difference then drives the control signals to the motors to change the actual altitude.

As you can see, if your quadcopter is too low, the difference between the **Desired Altitude** and the **Actual Altitude** will be positive, and the motor control will increase the voltage to the motors, increasing the altitude. If the quadcopter is too high, the difference between the **Desired Altitude** and the **Actual Altitude** will be negative, and the motor control will decrease the voltage to the motors, decreasing the altitude. If the **Desired Altitude** and the **Actual Altitude** are equal, then the difference between the two will be zero and the motor control will be held at its current value. Thus, the system stabilizes even if the components aren't perfect or if a wind comes along and blows the quadcopter up or down.

One application of the BeagleBone Black in this type of robotic project is to actually coordinate the measurement and control of the quadcopter's pitch, roll, yaw, and altitude. However, this is a very complex task and the details of its implementation are beyond the scope of this book. It is also difficult to do this with a processor that is running Linux, as Linux is not real time, and it might be off doing something else when it needs to respond to one of these control signals. This is especially true if the BeagleBone Black is busy processing images or GPS signals.

Some enterprising developers are working on developing flight controller code that can run on the BeagleBone Black, but be forewarned; this work is still very preliminary. This often includes modifying the Linux kernel, or basic operating system, to add real-time components. See `http://dev.ardupilot.com/wiki/building-for-beaglebone-black-on-linux/` for more information.

However, the BeagleBone Black can still be utilized in this type of robotic project. To do this, you will introduce another embedded processor to do the low-level control. Then you'll use the BeagleBone Black to manage the high-level tasks. For example, as in the sailboat example described in *Chapter 6, A Robot that Can Sail*, you can use the BeagleBone Black to coordinate GPS tracking, path planning, and long-range communications via ZigBee or Wireless LAN. This is the type of example that you'll learn in this chapter.

To do this project, you'll use a simple flight controller—one that focuses on the basics of flight. In this case, the communication between the BeagleBone Black and the flight controller is through the RC receiver control signals that are very similar to the servo control signals you learned about in *Chapter 5, Building a Robot that Can Walk*.

# Building the quadcopter

The first thing you'll need is the quadcopter itself. The most important component of the quadcopter is the flight controller board. There are several choices that can work, but this example is based on the Hobby King KK2.1.5 flight control board. Here is an image of the board:

The flight control board takes its flight inputs via a set of input signals that would normally come from an RC receiver to control the quadcopter, and then sends out control signals to the four motor controllers. You'll want a flight controller as it has built-in flight sensors, so it can handle the feedback control for the motors. The inputs from the BeagleBone Black will come in as electric commands to turn, bank, go forward, or increase/decrease the motor speed.

You can buy either an assembled quadcopter that uses the HobbyKing 2.1.5 board from HobbyKing at `www.hobbyking.com`, or you can buy the parts and assemble your own.

 If you'd like to assemble your own quadcopter, then there are a number of websites that document how to select the parts and assemble them. Try `http://www.instructables.com/id/Sturdy-Quadcopter-Build/?ALLSTEPS`, `http://robot-kingdom.com/build-your-own-quadcopter-beginner-guide-part-1/` or `http://flitetest.com/articles/Basic_Quadcopter_Tutorial_Talon_V2_KK2_Board_Plush_ESCs`.

The basic manual for this flight controller board is found at `www.dronetrest.com/uploads/db5290/428/769b8acab60b33aa.pdf`. Whether you are buying an assembled unit or building your own, it is a good idea to set up and fly your quadcopter first with an RC transmitter and receiver. This will give you a basic understanding of how the RC transmitter and receiver is connected to your quadcopter and some basic flight dynamics.

 Try the reference at `http://oddcopter.com/2012/07/24/setting-up-my-hobbyking-kk2-0-quadcopter-x/` or the video at `https://www.youtube.com/watch?v=qAyxyLMr6vg`.

Once you have it up and flying, you can add your BeagleBone Black to your project.

# Connecting the BeagleBone Black to the quadcopter

A nice thing about the KK 2.1.5 flight controller is that it has built-in flight sensors, so it can handle the feedback control for the motors. The other feature is that it has a screen and input buttons that will allow you to control the board manually during setup.

The control inputs come in as electric commands to turn, bank, go forward, or increase the altitude. Normally, these would come from your RC radio receiver. For this project, you'll disconnect these signals and insert the BeagleBone Black and the maestro servo controller to send the proper control signals. Here is a diagram that shows how you have to connect the BeagleBone Black, the servo controller, and the flight controller:

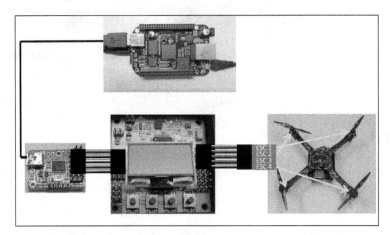

The following is a close-up image of the connections between the servo controller and the flight controller board:

Note that you need to use the foam that came with the flight controller as this will dampen the vibrations inherent in the system so that the sensors can make more accurate readings. Make sure you do not connect power to the servo controller; it does not need to supply power, it just sends the appropriate signals via the servo lines to the receiver input.

> As noted in *Chapter 5, Building a Robot that Can Walk*, you would probably want to put a powered USB hub between the servo controller and the BeagleBone Black. This will make the connection more stable and, if you later want to hook up a webcam and other accessories, provide reliable USB ports for those accessories.

# Controlling the quadcopter using the BeagleBone Black

Now you will use the BeagleBone Black to send commands to the servo controller, which will in turn control the flight controller board. To start this procedure, you'll need to add the RC battery to the quadcopter. This will power up the flight controller board. Connecting your battery should result in the following power-up screen on the flight controller board:

For this procedure, you'll start as if you are setting up a new flight controller board. If you have already set up the flight controller board with your radio, you will be able to skip down to step 7.

Here are the steps to set up your flight controller board to work with the BeagleBone Black:

1.  To start with, you'll need to set up the board to control your four-motor quadcopter. To do this, press the **MENU** key, press the **DOWN** button, and then the **Load Motor Layout** configuration button, as shown here:

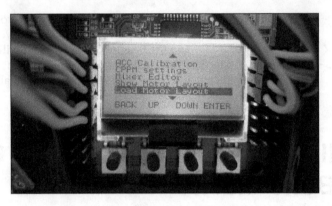

2.  Now you'll select the **QuadroCopter + mode** option, as shown in the following image:

3.  After you've selected this, the board will show you the layout of your motors. Make sure that your motors are configured with the direction of rotation as shown here:

4.  Now that the basic quadcopter is configured, you can test the sensors by pressing the **BACK** button until you get to the main menu. Press the **UP** key until you can select **Sensor Test**, as shown in the following image:

This will show the state of the sensors, which should look like this:

5. The next step is to calibrate the level sensors of the flight controller. From the main menu, select the **ACC Calibration** option as shown in the following image:

This will give you the details of the process, like this:

When you press **Continue**, the unit will calibrate the sensors as level, and then show you the following results:

6.  Press **Continue**, and you will return to the main menu.

7.  Now you can begin to send some signals through the servo controller to the board. To do this, go to the **Receiver Test** option of the main menu, as shown in the following image:

You should see this screen after selecting the **Receiver Test** option:

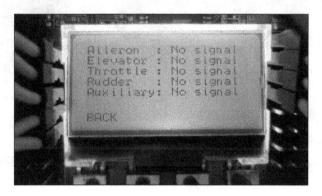

8. You'll now need to write some BeagleBone Black code to send some signals to the board. Open a PuTTY window on the BeagleBone Black, and enter this program:

```
ubuntu@arm: ~/quadcopter
File Edit Options Buffers Tools Python Help
#!/usr/bin/python
import serial
import time

def setAngle(ser, channel, angle):
    minAngle = 0.0
    maxAngle = 1000.0
    minTarget = 256.0
    maxTarget = 13120.0
    scaledValue = int((angle / ((maxAngle - minAngle) / (maxTarget - minTarget))) + minTarget)
    commandByte = chr(0x84)
    channelByte = chr(channel)
    lowTargetByte = chr(scaledValue & 0x7F)
    highTargetByte = chr((scaledValue >> 7) & 0x7F)
    command = commandByte + channelByte + lowTargetByte + highTargetByte
    ser.write(command)
    ser.flush()
def close(ser):
    ser.close()

ser = serial.Serial(port = "/dev/ttyACM0")
# Home position
setAngle(ser, 0,445)
setAngle(ser, 1,445)
setAngle(ser, 2,275)
setAngle(ser, 3,445)
setAngle(ser, 4,600)
servo = 0
while (servo != 8):
    servo = raw_input("servo number: ")
    angle = raw_input("input: ")
    setAngle(ser, int(servo), int(angle))

ser.close()

-UU-:----F1  simpleControl.py   All L1     (Python) -----------------------------------
For information about GNU Emacs and the GNU system, type C-h C-a.
```

This program should look familiar if you built the quadruped robot in *Chapter 5, Building a Robot that Can Walk*. The setAngle function, in this case, sets the value out of the servo controller for a single servo channel to a minimum of 275 and a maximum of 600. The middle of this range is 440.

9. Now run this program. This should send signals to the servo controller to center the servos, which in turn will send the signals to the flight controller board. The **Receiver Test** screen should now look like this:

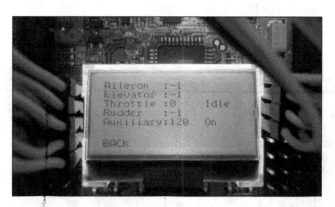

As you run the program and change the values of each servo, you should see that these values also change. For example, if you set the value of servo 0 to 275, the flight controller board should show the aileron set to a value that would turn it left, like this:

You now have the basic signals prepared to control the flight controller board. However, it is perhaps useful to have a graphics interface to send these commands to the flight controller board. Here is the listing of a graphical interface program to control the flight controller board, in four parts:

```
ubuntu@arm: ~/quadcopter
File Edit Options Buffers Tools Python Help
#!/usr/bin/python

from ttk import Frame, Label, Scale, Style
from Tkinter import *
from time import sleep
import serial

class Example(Frame):
    def __init__(self, parent):
        Frame.__init__(self, parent)
        self.parent = parent
        self.initUI()
    def initUI(self):
        self.parent.title("Quadcopter Control")
        self.style = Style()
        self.style.theme_use("default")
        self.pack(fill=BOTH, expand=1)
        scale1 = Scale(self, from_=275, to=675, length = 400,
                        orient=HORIZONTAL, command=self.onScale1)
        scale1.place(x=20, y=20)
        self.var1 = IntVar()
        self.label1 = Label(self, text=0, textvariable= self.var1)
        label1 = Label(text = "Forward/Reverse")
        label1.place(x = 40, y = 60)
        scale2 = Scale(self, from_=275, to=675, length = 400,
                        orient=HORIZONTAL, command=self.onScale2)
        scale2.place(x=20, y=100)
        self.var2 = IntVar()
        self.label2 = Label(self, text=0, textvariable= self.var2)
        label2 = Label(text = "left/right")
        label2.place(x = 40, y = 140)
        scale3 = Scale(self, from_=275, to=675, length = 400,
                        orient=HORIZONTAL, command=self.onScale3)
        scale3.place(x=20, y=180)
        self.var3 = IntVar()
        self.label3 = Label(self, text=0, textvariable= self.var3)
        label3 = Label(text = "Spin")
        label3.place(x = 40, y = 220)
        scale4 = Scale(self, from_=675, to=275, length = 400,
                        orient=VERTICAL, command=self.onScale4)
        scale4.place(x=500, y=20)
        self.var4 = IntVar()
        self.label4 = Label(self, text=0, textvariable= self.var4)
        label4 = Label(text = "Throttle")
-UU-:----F1  simpleUi.py     Top L1      (Python) -------------------------------
Beginning of buffer
```

The first part of the program contains a few includes, mostly for the graphical interface, but also for delay and serial control. The Example class sets up a simple interface with four slider bars to control the main four servo controls. It also sets up a quit command. Here is the listing for the second part of that class:

```
 ubuntu@arm: ~/quadcopter
File Edit Options Buffers Tools Python Help
        self.var1 = IntVar()
        self.label1 = Label(self, text=0, textvariable= self.var1)
        label1 = Label(text = "Forward/Reverse")
        label1.place(x = 40, y = 60)
        scale2 = Scale(self, from_=275, to=675, length = 400,
                       orient=HORIZONTAL, command=self.onScale2)
        scale2.place(x=20, y=100)
        self.var2 = IntVar()
        self.label2 = Label(self, text=0, textvariable= self.var2)
        label2 = Label(text = "left/right")
        label2.place(x = 40, y = 140)
        scale3 = Scale(self, from_=275, to=675, length = 400,
                       orient=HORIZONTAL, command=self.onScale3)
        scale3.place(x=20, y=180)
        self.var3 = IntVar()
        self.label3 = Label(self, text=0, textvariable= self.var3)
        label3 = Label(text = "Spin")
        label3.place(x = 40, y = 220)
        scale4 = Scale(self, from_=675, to=275, length = 400,
                       orient=VERTICAL, command=self.onScale4)
        scale4.place(x=500, y=20)
        self.var4 = IntVar()
        self.label4 = Label(self, text=0, textvariable= self.var4)
        label4 = Label(text = "Throttle")
        label4.place(x = 550, y = 100)
        quitButton = Button(self, text="Quit", command=self.quit)
        quitButton.place(x=50, y=450)
    def onScale1(self, val):
        v = int(float(val))
        robot.setAngle(0,v)
        self.var1.set(v)
    def onScale2(self, val):
        v = int(float(val))
        robot.setAngle(1,v)
        self.var2.set(v)
    def onScale3(self, val):
        v = int(float(val))
        robot.setAngle(3,v)
        self.var3.set(v)
    def onScale4(self, val):
        v = int(float(val))
        robot.setAngle(2,v)
        self.var4.set(v)

-UU-:----F1  simpleUi.py    18% L44    (Python) --------------------------------
```

The next listing shows the servo control functions, this time encapsulated in a class so as to make them easier to access, and the main function, which initializes everything and then starts the graphical user interface:

```
ubuntu@arm: ~/quadcopter
File Edit Options Buffers Tools Python Help

class PololuMicroMaestro(object):
    def __init__(self, port= "/dev/ttyACM0"):
        self.ser = serial.Serial(port = port)
    def setAngle(self, channel, angle):
        minAngle = 0.0
        maxAngle = 1000.0
        minTarget = 256.0
        maxTarget = 13120.0
        scaledValue = int((angle / ((maxAngle - minAngle) / (maxTarget - minTa\
rget))) + minTarget)
        commandByte = chr(0x84)
        channelByte = chr(channel)
        lowTargetByte = chr(scaledValue & 0x7F)
        highTargetByte = chr((scaledValue >> 7) & 0x7F)
        command = commandByte + channelByte + lowTargetByte + highTargetByte
        self.ser.write(command)
        self.ser.flush()
    def close(self):
        self.ser.close()

def task():
    label6 = Label(text = "Test")
    label6.place(x=200, y=350)
    root.after(2000, task)


if __name__ == '__main__':
    robot = PololuMicroMaestro()
    root = Tk()
    ex = Example(root)
    robot.setAngle(0,445)
    robot.setAngle(1,445)
    robot.setAngle(2,275)
    robot.setAngle(3,445)
    robot.setAngle(4,0)
    root.geometry("640x480+100+100")
    root.after(2000, task)
    root.mainloop()



-UU-:----F1  simpleUi.py     Bot L89     (Python) ------------------------
```

To run this program, since it is a graphical program, you'll need to use VNC server, as detailed in *Chapter 1, Preparing the BeagleBone Black*. But before that, you'll need to install a graphics package called `python-tk`. It allows you to build simple graphical user interfaces. Install it by typing `sudo apt-get install python-tk`. After you have installed the toolkit, run the program. Here is what the program will look like when it is running:

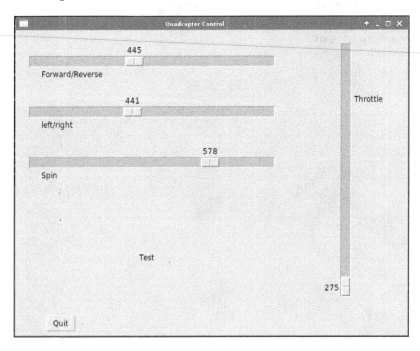

You can use this interface to control the flight controller board. One thing you will need to do (if you have not done previously) is using this interface to recalibrate your ESCs, adjust the stick sensitivity, and the other settings that you might want to tweak on the flight controller board.

 If you need to review the calibration procedure, visit `http://oddcopter.com/2012/07/24/setting-up-my-hobbyking-kk2-0-quadcopter-x/` or watch the video at `https://www.youtube.com/watch?v=qAyxyLMr6vg`.

Now your basic system is functional. You can use the BeagleBone Black to control the flight controller board and, in turn, your quadcopter.

# Summary

Now you have a quadcopter that can be controlled by the BeagleBone Black. However, your BeagleBone Black is still controlled via wired connection. In the next chapter, you'll use some of the techniques that you learned in the previous chapters to connect with the BeagleBone Black wirelessly and fly your quadcopter. Finally, you'll use a webcam to allow your BeagleBone Black to know about its world so that it can level and fly itself. You'll also use your knowledge of path planning and a GPS to fly the quadcopter autonomously.

# 11

# An Autonomous Quadcopter

You've now built your quadcopter, and you have the basic flight controller configured. But you'd like your quadcopter to be autonomous, that is, fly itself.

In this chapter you'll learn the following things:

- Controlling your quadcopter remotely from a computer using a joystick, through wireless computer signals
- Adding a webcam so that your quadcopter can do basic autonomous flight
- Adding a GPS device to make waypoint flights

 Through experience, I've learned that you will need to add some sort of propeller protection, as you'll very likely run into a wall or some other object more than once, and propellers can be expensive. There are some available at both `amazon.com` and `ebay.in`.

## Controlling quadcopter flight wirelessly

You've assembled your quadcopter and you can now control it via the BeagleBone Black. But there is still a LAN cable connected to your BeagleBone Black, which will make it difficult to fly very far. This section will show you how to get rid of that cable so that you can control your quadcopter without any wires.

One of the easiest ways to do this is to communicate with the BeagleBone Black on your quadcopter via wireless LAN. If you are using this technique, you'll need to configure a wireless access point for your BeagleBone Black quadcopter to connect to. There are several possible choices:

- You can use a wireless router as an access point to communicate between a computer and the BeagleBone Black on your quadcopter. To do this, simply connect a standard wireless router to the computer, and then configure it as a wireless access point using the directions for your specific router.

- You can configure a laptop computer as an access point to communicate with the BeagleBone Black on your quadcopter. If you are running Windows 7, try the directions at `http://lifehacker.com/5369381/turn-your-windows-7-pc-into-a-wireless-hotspot` or `http://www.firewall.cx/microsoft-knowledgebase/windows-xp-7-8/968-windows-7-access-point.html`. There are similar instructions for Windows 8 and XP; just do an Internet search. If you have an Ubuntu Linux machine, try `http://www.cyberciti.biz/faq/debian-ubuntu-linux-setting-wireless-access-point/` or `http://www.howtogeek.com/116409/how-to-turn-your-ubuntu-laptop-into-a-wireless-access-point/`.

- You can use a second BeagleBone Black configured as an access point to communicate with the BeagleBone Black on your quadcopter. To use this method, follow the directions at `http://fleshandmachines.wordpress.com/2012/10/04/wifi-acces-point-on-beaglebone-with-dhcp/`.

**Just a word of warning**

This can be a bit tricky to get to work, and if you use this configuration and you want to take your quadcopter outside, you'll need an HDMI or DVI screen for your control computer.

Once you have the access point configured, use the instructions from *Chapter 1, Preparing the BeagleBone Black*, to configure the wireless LAN connection on the BeagleBone Black that is on your quadcopter. You'll then need to mount the BeagleBone Black, the powered USB hub, and a battery that can supply both with power onto the quadcopter. You can use two small USB batteries, one for the BeagleBone Black and one for the powered USB hub, to power both of these for your quadcopter configuration.

Once you have all of the previously mentioned equipment configured, you can run the control program introduced at the end of the last chapter using a VNC server configuration. Doing this will allow you basic control of the quadcopter wirelessly. You should be able to actually fly your quadcopter by running this program remotely using VNC viewer and the keyboard and sliding controls. However, it would be easier to control your quadcopter using a game controller.

# Adding a game controller to your system

The software introduced in the last chapter is functional, but not very practical. What you will need is a controller that has more immediate control of the different servos. Perhaps the most practical is a game controller that has two joysticks and several additional buttons. This will make flying your quadcopter through the BeagleBone Black much easier.

To add the game controller, you'll need to first find a game controller that can connect to your computer. If you are using Microsoft Windows as the OS on the host computer, pretty much any USB controller that can connect to a PC will work. The same type of controller also works if you are using Linux for the remote computer. In fact, you can use another BeagleBone Black as the remote computer.

Since the joystick will be connected to the remote computer, you'll need to run two programs: one on the remote computer and one on the BeagleBone Black on the quadcopter. You'll also need a way to communicate between them. In the following example, you'll use the wireless LAN interface and a client-server model of communication. You'll run the server program on the remote computer, and the client program on the BeagleBone Black on the quadcopter.

>  For an excellent tutorial of this type of model and how it is used in a gaming application, see http://www.raywenderlich.com/38732/multiplayer-game-programming-for-teens-with-python.

Once you have the controller connected, you'll need to create a Python program on the BeagleBone Black that will take the signals sent from the client and send the correct signals to the servo controllers. This is the client program. But before you do that, you'll need to install the libraries that will allow this program to work. The first is a library called pygame. Install this library by typing sudo apt-get install python-pygame. Then you'll need a LAN communication layer library called PodSixNet. This will allow the two applications to communicate. To install this library, follow the instructions at http://mccormick.cx/projects/PodSixNet/.

Now you are ready to create the client program on the BeagleBone Black on the quadcopter. Here is the first listing of the program:

```
ubuntu@arm: ~/quadcopter                                    _  □  X
File Edit Options Buffers Tools Python Help
import pygame
import math
from PodSixNet.Connection import ConnectionListener, connection
from time import sleep
import serial

class PololuMicroMaestro(object):
    def __init__(self, port= "/dev/ttyACM0"):
        self.ser = serial.Serial(port = port)
    def setAngle(self, channel, angle):
        minAngle = 0.0
        maxAngle = 1000.0
        minTarget = 256.0
        maxTarget = 13120.0
        scaledValue = int((angle / ((maxAngle - minAngle) / (maxTarget - minTar\
get))) + minTarget)
        commandByte = chr(0x84)
        channelByte = chr(channel)
        lowTargetByte = chr(scaledValue & 0x7F)
        highTargetByte = chr((scaledValue >> 7) & 0x7F)
        command = commandByte + channelByte + lowTargetByte + highTargetByte
        self.ser.write(command)
        self.ser.flush()
    def close(self):
        self.ser.close()

-UU-:----F1  QUAD_client.py   Top L1     (Python) ----------------------------
Beginning of buffer
```

The first part of the program is a Python class that sends the commands to the servo controller. If you built the quadruped robot in *Chapter 5, Building a Robot that Can Walk*, this code should look familiar. The following is the second part of this code:

```
ubuntu@arm: ~/quadcopter
File Edit Options Buffers Tools Python Help

class QuadGame(ConnectionListener):
    def Network_close(self, data):
        exit()
    def Network_gamepad(self, data):
        global throttle
        global rudder
        global elevator
        global aileron

        global robot

        if data["type"] == 10:
            #print "Pressed button "
            #print data["info"]["button"]
            if data["info"]["button"] == 0:
                throttle = throttle + 10
                if throttle > 675:
                    throttle = 675
                print "Throttle up to"
                print throttle
                robot.setAngle(2, throttle)
            if data["info"]["button"] == 1:
                throttle = throttle - 10
                if throttle < 275:
                    throttle = 275
                print "Throttle down to"
                print throttle
                robot.setAngle(2, throttle)
            if data["info"]["button"] == 5:
                rudder = rudder + 10
                if rudder > 675:
                    rudder = 675
                print "Rudder right to"
                print rudder
                robot.setAngle(3, rudder)
            if data["info"]["button"] == 4:
                rudder = rudder - 10
                if rudder < 275:
                    rudder = 275
                print "Rudder left to"
                print rudder
                robot.setAngle(3, rudder)
            if data["info"]["button"] == 9:
-UU-:----F1   QUAD_client.py   15% L47   (Python) -----------------------------
```

In this section, you'll create a class called QuadGame. This class will take the inputs from the game controller connected to the server and turn them into commands that will be sent to the servo controller, then to the flight controller to control your quadcopter.

Here is a table of the joystick controls and their corresponding quadcopter controls:

| Joystick control | Quadcopter control |
|---|---|
| Button 10 | Throttle up |
| Button 1 | Throttle down |
| Button 5 | Rudder right |
| Button 4 | Rudder left |
| Button 9 | All controls to arm position |
| Button 8 | All controls to disarm position |
| Button 6 | Center all controls |
| Button 7 | Center all controls |
| Joystick 1 Up/Down | Aileron right/left |
| Joystick 2 Up/Down | Elevator forward/backward |

Here is the second part of the QuadGame class:

```python
        if data["info"]["button"] == 9:
            print "ARMING"
            rudder = 445
            throttle = 275
            robot.setAngle(2, 275) # Throttle down
            robot.setAngle(3, 355) # Rudder left
            sleep(.1)
            robot.setAngle(2, throttle)
            robot.setAngle(3, rudder)
        if data["info"]["button"] == 8:
            print "DISARMING"
            rudder = 445
            throttle = 275
            robot.setAngle(2, 275) # Throttle down
            robot.setAngle(3, 535) # Rudder right
            sleep(.1)
            robot.setAngle(2, throttle)
            robot.setAngle(3, rudder)
        if data["info"]["button"] == 6:
            print "CENTERING"
            rudder = 445
            throttle = 275
            elevator = 445
            aileron = 445
            robot.setAngle(0, elevator)
            robot.setAngle(1, aileron)
            robot.setAngle(2, throttle)
            robot.setAngle(3, rudder)
        if data["info"]["button"] == 7:
            print "CENTERING"
            rudder = 445
            throttle = 275
            elevator = 445
            aileron = 445
            robot.setAngle(0, elevator)
            robot.setAngle(1, aileron)
            robot.setAngle(2, throttle)
            robot.setAngle(3, rudder)
    if data["type"] == 9:
        #print "Hat state is "
        #print data["info"]["value"]
        if data["info"]["value"][0] == -1:
            aileron = aileron - 10
            if aileron < 275:
```

This class continues the control part of the code, implementing all the different buttons and joysticks on the controller. The following screenshot shows the final section of the joystick controller part of the client program:

```
if data["type"] == 9:
    #print "Hat state is "
    #print data["info"]["value"]
    if data["info"]["value"][0] == -1:
        aileron = aileron - 10
        if aileron < 275:
            aileron = 275
        print "Aileron left to"
        print aileron
        robot.setAngle(1, aileron)
    if data["info"]["value"][0] == 1:
        aileron = aileron + 10
        if aileron > 675:
            aileron = 675
        print "Aileron right to"
        print aileron
        robot.setAngle(1, aileron)
    if data["info"]["value"][1] == 1:
        elevator = elevator - 10
        if elevator < 275:
            elevator = 275
        print "Elevator back to"
        print elevator
        robot.setAngle(0, elevator)
    if data["info"]["value"][1] == -1:
        elevator = elevator + 10
        if elevator > 675:
            elevator = 675
        print "Elevator forward to"
        print elevator
        robot.setAngle(0, elevator)
def __init__(self):
    address=raw_input("Address of Server: ")
    try:
        if not address:
            host, port="localhost", 8000
        else:
            host,port=address.split(":")
        self.Connect((host, int(port)))
    except:
        print "Error Connecting to Server"
        print "Usage:", "host:port"
        print "e.g.", "localhost:31425"
        exit()
-UU-:**--F1   QUAD client.py   64% L138   (Python) -----
```

This final part of the code completes the QuadGame class, implementing the rest of the button and joystick controls. It also includes the code to initialize the interface layer, including how the user will specify the server machine.

Now here is the final piece of the code:

```
ubuntu@arm: ~/quadcopter
File Edit Options Buffers Tools Python Help
        try:
            if not address:
                host, port="localhost", 8000
            else:
                host,port=address.split(":")
            self.Connect((host, int(port)))
        except:
            print "Error Connecting to Server"
            print "Usage:", "host:port"
            print "e.g.", "localhost:31425"
            exit()
        print "Quad client started"
        self.running=False
        while not self.running:
            self.Pump()
            connection.Pump()
            sleep(0.01)

global throttle
global rudder
global elevator
global aileron

global robot

throttle = 275
rudder = 445
elevator = 445
aileron = 445

robot = PololuMicroMaestro()

robot.setAngle(0,445)
robot.setAngle(1,445)
robot.setAngle(2,275)
robot.setAngle(3,445)
robot.setAngle(4,0)

bg=QuadGame() # __init__ is called right here
while 1:
    if bg.update()==1:
        break
bg.finished()
-UU-:**--F1  QUAD_client.py  Bot L181   (Python) ----------------------------
```

This final piece of code sets the initial values of the servo controller, and thus the flight controller, to their center location. Then it initializes the game loop, which loops while taking the inputs and sends them to the servo controller and further onto the flight controller.

You'll also need a server program running on the remote computer that will take the signals from the game controller and send them to the client. You'll be writing this code in Python using Python Version 2.7, which can be installed from here. Additionally, you'll need to install the pygame library. If you are using Linux on the remote computer, then type sudo apt-get install python-pygame. If you are using Microsoft Windows on the remote machine, then follow the instructions at http://www.pygame.org/download.shtml.

You'll also need the LAN communication layer described previously. You can find a version that will run on Microsoft Windows or Linux at http://mccormick.cx/projects/PodSixNet/. The following is a listing of the server code, in two parts:

```
Python 2.7.8: flightserver - C:/Python27/flightserver
File Edit Format Run Options Windows Help
import PodSixNet.Server
from pygame import *
from time import sleep
init()
from time import sleep
class ClientChannel(PodSixNet.Channel.Channel):
    def Network(self, data):
        print data
    def Close(self):
        self._server.close(self.gameid)
class BoxesServer(PodSixNet.Server.Server):

    channelClass = ClientChannel
    def __init__(self, *args, **kwargs):
        PodSixNet.Server.Server.__init__(self, *args, **kwargs)
        self.games = []
        self.queue = None
        self.currentIndex=0
    def Connected(self, channel, addr):
        print 'new connection:', channel
        if self.queue==None:
            self.currentIndex+=1
            channel.gameid=self.currentIndex
            self.queue=Game(channel, self.currentIndex)
    def close(self, gameid):
        try:
            game = [a for a in self.games if a.gameid==gameid][0]
            game.player0.Send({"action":"close"})
        except:
            pass
    def tick(self):
        if self.queue != None:
            sleep(.05)
            for e in event.get():
                self.queue.player0.Send({"action":"gamepad", "type":e.type, "in
        self.Pump()
class Game:
    def __init__(self, player0, currentIndex):
        #initialize the players including the one who started the game
        self.player0=player0

#Setup and init joystick
j=joystick.Joystick(0)
j.init()

#Check init status
if j.get_init() == 1: print "Joystick is initialized"
```

This first part creates three classes:

- The first, `ClientChannel`, establishes a communication channel for your project
- The second, `BoxServer`, sets up a server so that you can communicate the joystick action to the BeagleBone Black on the quadcopter
- Finally, the `Game` class just initializes a game that contains everything you'll need

Here is the second part of the server code:

```
Python 2.7.8: flightserver - C:/Python27/flightserver
File  Edit  Format  Run  Options  Windows  Help
                sleep(.05)
                for e in event.get():
                    self.queue.player0.Send({"action":"gamepad", "type":e.type, "in
        self.Pump()
class Game:
    def __init__(self, player0, currentIndex):
        #initialize the players including the one who started the game
        self.player0=player0

#Setup and init joystick
j=joystick.Joystick(0)
j.init()

#Check init status
if j.get_init() == 1: print "Joystick is initialized"

#Get and print joystick ID
print "Joystick ID: ", j.get_id()

#Get and print joystick name
print "Joystick Name: ", j.get_name()

#Get and print number of axes
print "No. of axes: ", j.get_numaxes()

#Get and print number of trackballs
print "No. of trackballs: ", j.get_numballs()

#Get and print number of buttons
print "No. of buttons: ", j.get_numbuttons()

#Get and print number of hat controls
print "No. of hat controls: ", j.get_numhats()


print "STARTING SERVER ON LOCALHOST"
# try:
address=raw_input("Host:Port (localhost:8000): ")
if not address:
    host, port="localhost", 8000
else:
    host,port=address.split(":")
boxesServe = BoxesServer(localaddr=(host, int(port)))

while True:
    boxesServe.tick()
    sleep(0.01)
```

The preceding part of the code initializes the joystick so that all the controls can be sent to the quadcopter's BeagleBone Black.

You may want your quadcopter to take flight quite a distance from your controlling computer. Wireless has a maximum range of 300 feet, so if you are looking for long flights, you'll need a technology that can extend the wireless connection much further. In *Chapter 6*, *A Robot that Can Sail*, you learned how to implement an XBee communication link.

By sending characters across the XBee interface, you can create an application on the host computer that can send commands based on the game controller input. You'll need to replace the LAN interface code in the previous example with a serial interface.

# Adding a webcam for autonomous flight

At this point, your quadcopter is controlled by you via a wireless interface. However, you might want to experiment with allowing your quadcopter to control its own flight. Here you'll learn some basic concepts of **Proportional-Integrative-Derivative (PID)** control to begin exploring this space. There won't be complete or explicit instructions. That would take a book in and of itself. But you can at least get started.

To allow your quadcopter to fly itself, it will need some information about the world around it. One possible way to provide this is to use a webcam and some markers in your flight area. If you followed the instructions in *Chapter 1*, *Preparing the BeagleBone Black*, you should have installed all of the software you need in order to add a webcam and view the world around you.

You'll also need to review the concepts from *Chapter 4*, *Vision and Image Processing*, for your robotic project. In particular, what you'll want to do is control your quadcopter just as you controlled your wheeled vehicle to follow the colored ball. However, you're going to use an advanced control technique, utilizing the feedback control technique used by the flight controller board to allow it to provide stable flight. In this case, you'll use the webcam and the colored ball to set a position and PID code implemented in Python on the BeagleBone Black to control the larger up and down movements of the quadcopter. You can use this same technique to control the forward/backward and side-to-side position of the quadcopter.

To understand PID control, you'll need to recall the basic feedback loop you discovered in *Chapter 10, A Quadcopter*. Here is the diagram of the feedback loop from that chapter:

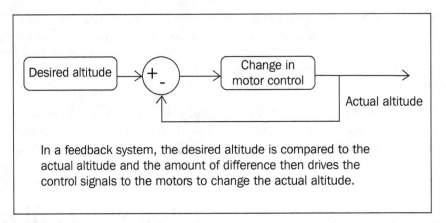

In this case, the desired altitude will be in the middle of the webcam window that captures the colored ball. The actual altitude will be in the center of the color blob in the webcam window. These will be compared and the BeagleBone Black on the quadcopter will adjust the throttle to either increase or decrease the value to compensate for the difference. This is well explained in the preceding diagram.

Here is the first part of the code that shows how this simple example might work:

```python
#!/usr/bin/python
import serial
import time
import cv2.cv as cv
import time
import subprocess

def setAngle(ser, channel, angle):
    minAngle = 0.0
    maxAngle = 1000.0
    minTarget = 256.0
    maxTarget = 13120.0
    scaledValue = int((angle / ((maxAngle - minAngle) / (maxTarget - minTarget))) + minTarget)
    commandByte = chr(0x84)
    channelByte = chr(channel)
    lowTargetByte = chr(scaledValue & 0x7F)
    highTargetByte = chr((scaledValue >> 7) & 0x7F)
    command = commandByte + channelByte + lowTargetByte + highTargetByte
    ser.write(command)
    ser.flush()
def close(ser):
    ser.close()

ser = serial.Serial(port = "/dev/ttyACM0")
capture = cv.CaptureFromCAM(0)
cv.SetCaptureProperty(capture, 3, 360)
cv.SetCaptureProperty(capture, 4, 240)
# Home position
setAngle(ser, 0,445)
setAngle(ser, 1,445)
setAngle(ser, 2,275)
setAngle(ser, 3,445)
setAngle(ser, 4,600)
throttle = 275
while True:
    img = cv.QueryFrame(capture)
    cv.Smooth(img,img,cv.CV_BLUR,3)
    hue_img = cv.CreateImage(cv.GetSize(img), 8, 3)
    cv.CvtColor(img, hue_img, cv.CV_BGR2HSV)
    threshold_img = cv.CreateImage(cv.GetSize(hue_img), 8, 1)
    cv.InRangeS(hue_img, (38,120, 60), (75, 255, 255), threshold_img)
    storage = cv.CreateMemStorage(0)
    contour = cv.FindContours(threshold_img, storage, cv.CV_RETR_CCOMP, cv.CV_CHAIN_APPROX_SIMPLE)
    points = []
    cx = 0
```

-UU-:----F1   **simpleControl.py**    Top L1      (Python) ------------------------
Beginning of buffer

The first part of the code has the includes needed by the program, and the functions needed to control the servo controller which in turn will control the flight controller. Here is the second part of the code:

```python
setAngle(ser, 3,445)
setAngle(ser, 4,600)
throttle = 275
while True:
    img = cv.QueryFrame(capture)
    cv.Smooth(img,img,cv.CV_BLUR,3)
    hue_img = cv.CreateImage(cv.GetSize(img), 8, 3)
    cv.CvtColor(img, hue_img, cv.CV_BGR2HSV)
    threshold_img = cv.CreateImage(cv.GetSize(hue_img), 8, 1)
    cv.InRangeS(hue_img, (38,120, 60), (75, 255, 255), threshold_img)
    storage = cv.CreateMemStorage(0)
    contour = cv.FindContours(threshold_img, storage, cv.CV_RETR_CCOMP, cv.CV_CHAIN_APPROX_SIMPLE)
    points = []
    cx = 0
    cy = 0
    while contour:
        rect = cv.BoundingRect(list(contour))
        contour = contour.h_next()
        size = (rect[2] * rect[3])
        if size > 100:
            pt1 = (rect[0], rect[1])
            pt2 = (rect[0] + rect[2], rect[1] + rect[3])
            cx = rect[0]
            cy = rect[1]
            cv.Rectangle(img, pt1, pt2, (38, 160, 60))
    cv.ShowImage("Colour Tracking", img)
    if cy > 120:
        throttle = throttle - 10
        if throttle < 275:
            throttle = 275
        print "Throttle down to"
        print throttle
        setAngle(ser, 2, throttle)
    if cy < 120:
        throttle = throttle + 10
        if throttle > 675:
            throttle = 675
        print "Throttle up to"
        print throttle
        setAngle(ser, 2, throttle)
    if cv.WaitKey(10) == 27:
        break

ser.close()
```

This second part of the program is a `while` loop that takes an image, then finds out in which direction the colored ball is. If the ball is below the center of the image, or in the lower part of the screen, the throttle will be increased by 10. If the ball is in the upper part of the window, the throttle will be decreased by 10. This value—the amount by which the throttle is decreased or increased—will establish the stability of the control. If the value is too large, then the quadcopter will go up and down violently as it tries to find the ball. If the value is too small, then it will take a very long time to put the ball on the screen.

This simple adjustment, that is, increasing or decreasing the throttle based on the position of the ball, is called **proportional control**. If the value is set correctly, your quadcopter will level with the ball, but it might take a great deal of time to do this. There is a more efficient algorithm to more quickly center on the ball. Here is a diagram of this type of control:

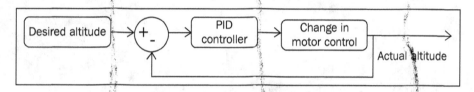

Here you take the desired altitude and compare it to the actual altitude, but instead of setting the change in motor control simply on this difference, you'll include both the derivative (how fast the change in the value occurs) and the integrative (how long the change is taking) into account as you adjust the throttle.

 To understand more about PID controllers, see the tutorials at http://www.csimn.com/CSI_pages/PIDforDummies.html or http://en.wikipedia.org/wiki/PID_controller.

The second tutorial is particularly useful because it discusses not only how the PID controller works, but also how to tune the setting to get a stable control loop.

Here is the first part of some example code that is similar to the previous code, apart from the fact that it adds the integrative and derivative control functions to your program:

```python
ubuntu@arm: ~/quadcopter
File Edit Options Buffers Tools Python Help
#!/usr/bin/python
import serial
import time
import cv2.cv as cv
import time
import subprocess

def setAngle(ser, channel, angle):
    minAngle = 0.0
    maxAngle = 1000.0
    minTarget = 256.0
    maxTarget = 13120.0
    scaledValue = int((angle / ((maxAngle - minAngle) / (maxTarget - minTarget))) + minTarget)
    commandByte = chr(0x84)
    channelByte = chr(channel)
    lowTargetByte = chr(scaledValue & 0x7F)
    highTargetByte = chr((scaledValue >> 7) & 0x7F)
    command = commandByte + channelByte + lowTargetByte + highTargetByte
    ser.write(command)
    ser.flush()
def close(ser):
    ser.close()

def updatePID(current_value,set_point,Kp,Ki,Kd,Integrator,Derivator,Integrator_max,Integrator_min):
    error = set_point - current_value
    P_value = Kp * error
    D_value = Kd * (error - Derivator)
    Derivator = error
    Integrator = Integrator + error
    if Integrator > Integrator_max:
        Integrator = Integrator_max
    elif Integrator < Integrator_min:
        Integrator = Integrator_min
    I_value = Integrator * Ki
    PID = P_value + I_value + D_value
    return PID

ser = serial.Serial(port = "/dev/ttyACM0")
capture = cv.CaptureFromCAM(0)
cv.SetCaptureProperty(capture, 3, 360)
cv.SetCaptureProperty(capture, 4, 240)
# Home position
setAngle(ser, 0,445)
setAngle(ser, 1,445)
setAngle(ser, 2,275)
-UU-:**--F1  simpleControl.py  Top L25   (Python) --------------------------
```

In the preceding section of code, the key addition is the updatePID function. This function takes the current location and the desired location, and calculates an error value. It then uses the PID concepts to apply a proportional, integrative, and derivative correction factor. This returns a PID value that will change the set point of the throttle.

Here is the second part of the code that implements the PID mechanism:

```
ubuntu@arm: ~/quadcopter
File Edit Options Buffers Tools Python Help
throttle = 275
error = 0
Kp = 2.0
Ki = 0.0
Kd = 1.0
Integrator = 0
Derivator = 0
Integrator_max = 500
Integrator_min = -500
while True:
    img = cv.QueryFrame(capture)
    cv.Smooth(img,img,cv.CV_BLUR,3)
    hue_img = cv.CreateImage(cv.GetSize(img), 8, 3)
    cv.CvtColor(img, hue_img, cv.CV_BGR2HSV)
    threshold_img = cv.CreateImage(cv.GetSize(hue_img), 8, 1)
    cv.InRangeS(hue_img, (38,120, 60), (75, 255, 255), threshold_img)
    storage = cv.CreateMemStorage(0)
    contour = cv.FindContours(threshold_img, storage, cv.CV_RETR_CCOMP, cv.CV_CHAIN_APPROX_SIMPLE)
    points = []
    cx = 0
    cy = 0
    while contour:
        rect = cv.BoundingRect(list(contour))
        contour = contour.h_next()
        size = (rect[2] * rect[3])
        if size > 100:
            pt1 = (rect[0], rect[1])
            pt2 = (rect[0] + rect[2], rect[1] + rect[3])
            cx = rect[0]
            cy = rect[1]
            cv.Rectangle(img, pt1, pt2, (38, 160, 60))
    cv.ShowImage("Colour Tracking", img)
    if cy == 0:
        throttle = 675
    else:
        PID = updatePID(cy, 120, Kp, Ki, Kd, Integrator, Derivator, Integrator_max, Integrator_min)
        throttle = throttle - PID
        if throttle > 675:
            throttle = 675
        if throttle < 275:
            throttle = 275
    print throttle
    setAngle(ser, 2, throttle)
    if cv.WaitKey(10) == 27:
        break
-UU-:**--F1   simpleControl.py   49% L70     (Python) -----------------------------------
```

Just before the `while` loop, you'll need to initialize the variables associated with the PID controller. The `Kp` value sets the amount the proportional value affects the control, the `Ki` value sets the amount the integrative value affects the control, and the `Kd` value sets the amount the derivative value affects the control. You'll need to tweak these values based on the performance of your controller. Each time you call `updatePID` through the loop, this function will return a new value to change the throttle.

# Adding GPS for autonomous flight

Another way to introduce autonomy to your quadcopter is to use the GPS capability you learned in *Chapter 7, Using GPS for Navigation*, to give direction to your sailboat; to control your quadcopter autonomously. You can use the GPS to plan new waypoints and path planning to fly your quadcopter to specific locations. You can use the altitude from the GPS to control the height of your flight, although this might result in some rough landings as it rarely gives the kind of resolution to bring your quadcopter down softly. I often use a sonar sensor, similar to the one covered in *Chapter 3, Adding Sensors to Your Tracked Vehicle*, to sense the ground and land the quadcopter softly.

# Summary

Well, that's it! You should have lots of different robots now that can do a number of amazing things. Hopefully this is just the beginning; the rest is left to your imagination and budget. Feel free to explore, although you will almost certainly go through a wrecked robot or two. But that is a small price for the kind of experiences you will have!

# Index

# Index

**D**

Dagu Rover 5 Tracked Chassis  33
DC motors
  about  34
  controlling, with Python program  162-172
Debian  9
Degrees of Freedom (DOF)  93
Desired Altitude  179
distance
  calculating  141-143
distance sensors
  adding  51
  IR sensor  56
  sonar sensor  52
dynamic IP address  10
dynamic path planning, robot
  about  60
  obstacles, avoiding  64-68
  path planning  61-63
  references  63

**E**

Electronic Speed Controllers (ESC)  160
Espeak  23
external computer
  connecting to  10
EZ Tops
  URL  159

**F**

feedback control  179

**G**

game controller
  adding, to system  197-205
General-Purpose Input/Output (GPIO)  7
Global Positioning System. *See* GPS
GND pin  146
go_backward function  166
go_down function  166
go_forward function  166
go_left function  166
go_right function  166

go_up function  166
GPIO pins
  URL  34
GPS
  about  129
  adding, for autonomous quadcopter
    flight  212
  communicating with  134-139
  connecting, to BeagleBone Black  132, 133
  tutorial  129-132
GPS information
  parsing  139-141

**H**

hardware
  building, for ROV  157-160
haversine formula
  about  141
  URL  142
Hitec servos  95
Hue (color), Saturation, and Value (HSV)  78

**I**

inexpensive sonar sensor
  adding  53-56
  issues  54
Infrared sensor. *See* IR sensor
irons  154
IR sensor
  about  56-60
  connecting, to BeagleBone Black  57

**J**

joystick controls  200

**L**

latitude  141
Linux
  program, creating for quadruped
    control  106-109
longitude  141
long LAN
  used, for connecting to BeagleBone
    Black  172-175

## R

**Real VNC**
about 12
URL 12
**Red, Green, and Blue (RGB) 78**
**Remotely Operated Vehicle.** *See* ROV
**robot**
dynamic path planning 60
**ROV**
about 157
component 159
hardware, building for 157-160
**RV pin 147**
**RX/TX interface 134**
**RX/TX port 135, 140**

## S

**sailboat platform**
building 114, 115
**sailing**
about 151-155
references 152
rudder setting 152
sail setting 152
URL 152
**Secure Shell Hyperterminal (SSH) 11**
**sensor data**
obtaining, from analog wind speed
sensor 148-151
**sensors**
basics 51
**servo controller**
communicating, via PC 102, 103
connecting, to BeagleBone Black 103-106
used, for controlling servos 99-101
**servomotors**
working 94
**servos**
controlling, from program 118, 119
controlling, with BeagleBone Black 115-117
controlling, with servo controller 99-101
**shutdown function 166**
**sonar sensor**
about 52

adding, to project 53
USB-ProxSonar-EZ 53
**sound**
creating 20-22
installing 19
recording 20-22
**speech recognition, BeagleBone Black**
accuracy, improving 27-29
installing 23-27
URL 28
**sphinxbase 23**
**static IP address 10**
**stop function 166**

## T

**tack 155**
**TightVNC server 12**
**Tkinter**
URL 168
**TMP pin 146**
**torque 95**
**tracked platform**
selecting 33, 34
**triangulation 130**

## U

**Ubuntu 9**
**underwater ROV**
URL 157

## V

**vision library**
installing 16-18
**vision system**
colored objects, finding 77-80
colored objects, following 81-83
movement, finding 83-88
**VNC server 11**
**voice commands**
issuing, to quadruped 110, 111
motor control, accessing via 47-50
responding to 29, 30

# W

**webcam**
  adding, for autonomous quadcopter
       flight  205-211
  connecting, to BeagleBone Black  71-74
**Windows manager**
  installing  11, 12
**wireless LAN**
  quadcopter flight, controlling via  195, 196

# X

**XBee**
  about  120
  URL  120
**Xfce  11**

# Z

**ZigBee**
  about  119, 120
  tutorial  120, 121

## Thank you for buying
# Mastering BeagleBone Robotics

# About Packt Publishing

Packt, pronounced 'packed', published its first book, *Mastering phpMyAdmin for Effective MySQL Management*, in April 2004, and subsequently continued to specialize in publishing highly focused books on specific technologies and solutions.

Our books and publications share the experiences of your fellow IT professionals in adapting and customizing today's systems, applications, and frameworks. Our solution-based books give you the knowledge and power to customize the software and technologies you're using to get the job done. Packt books are more specific and less general than the IT books you have seen in the past. Our unique business model allows us to bring you more focused information, giving you more of what you need to know, and less of what you don't.

Packt is a modern yet unique publishing company that focuses on producing quality, cutting-edge books for communities of developers, administrators, and newbies alike. For more information, please visit our website at www.packtpub.com.

# About Packt Open Source

In 2010, Packt launched two new brands, Packt Open Source and Packt Enterprise, in order to continue its focus on specialization. This book is part of the Packt Open Source brand, home to books published on software built around open source licenses, and offering information to anybody from advanced developers to budding web designers. The Open Source brand also runs Packt's Open Source Royalty Scheme, by which Packt gives a royalty to each open source project about whose software a book is sold.

# Writing for Packt

We welcome all inquiries from people who are interested in authoring. Book proposals should be sent to author@packtpub.com. If your book idea is still at an early stage and you would like to discuss it first before writing a formal book proposal, then please contact us; one of our commissioning editors will get in touch with you.

We're not just looking for published authors; if you have strong technical skills but no writing experience, our experienced editors can help you develop a writing career, or simply get some additional reward for your expertise.

## BeagleBone for Secret Agents

ISBN: 978-1-78398-604-0          Paperback: 162 pages

Browse anonymously, communicate secretly, and create custom security solutions with open source software, the BeagleBone Black, and cryptographic hardware

1. Interface with cryptographic hardware to add security to your embedded project, securing you from external threats.

2. Use and build applications with trusted anonymity and security software such as Tor and GPG to defend your privacy and confidentiality.

3. Work with low-level I/O on BeagleBone Black such as I2C, GPIO, and serial interfaces to create custom hardware applications.

## Building a Home Security System with BeagleBone

ISBN: 978-1-78355-960-2          Paperback: 120 pages

Build your own high-tech alarm system at a fraction of the cost

1. Build your own state-of-the-art security system.

2. Monitor your system from any place where you can receive e-mails.

3. Add control of other systems such as sprinklers and gates.

4. Save thousands on monitoring and rental fees.

Please check **www.PacktPub.com** for information on our titles

## BeagleBone Home Automation

ISBN: 978-1-78328-573-0      Paperback: 178 pages

Live your sophisticated dream with home automation using BeagleBone

1. Practical approach to home automation using BeagleBone; starting from the very basics of GPIO control and progressing up to building a complete home automation solution.

2. Covers the operating principles of a range of useful environment sensors, including their programming and integration to the server application.

3. Easy-to-follow approach with electronics schematics, wiring diagrams, and controller code, all broken down into manageable and easy-to-understand sections.

## Rapid BeagleBoard Prototyping with MATLAB and Simulink

ISBN: 978-1-84969-604-3      Paperback: 152 pages

Leverage the power of BeagleBoard to develop and deploy practical embedded projects

1. Develop and validate your own embedded audio/video applications rapidly with BeagleBoard.

2. Create embedded Linux applications on a pure Windows PC.

3. Full of illustrations, diagrams, and tips for rapid BeagleBoard Prototyping with clear, step-by-step instructions and hands-on examples.

Please check **www.PacktPub.com** for information on our titles

www.ingramcontent.com/pod-product-compliance
Lightning Source LLC
Chambersburg PA
CBHW082118070326
40690CB00049B/3649